Impossible
Loves

Impossible
Loves

Don Cupitt

POLEBRIDGE PRESS
Santa Rosa, California

'Prayer' is taken from "Mean Time" by Carol Ann Duffy published by Anvil Press Poetry in 1993. Used by permission.

Cover and interior design by Robaire Ream
Cover photograph by Robaire Ream

Library of Congress Cataloging-in-Publication Data

Cupitt, Don.
  Impossible loves / Don Cupitt.
      p. cm.
  Includes bibliographical references and index.
  ISBN-13: 978-1-59815-001-8
  1. Memory--Religious aspects--Christianity. 2. Regret--Religious aspects--Christianity. 3. Possibility--Religious aspects--Christianity. I. Title.
  BV4597.565.C87 2007
  218--dc22
                                    2007032134

Contents

S ome days, although we cannot pray, a prayer
utters itself. So, a woman will lift
her head from the sieve of her hands and stare
at the minims sung by a tree, a sudden gift.

Some nights, although we are faithless, the truth
enters our hearts, that small familiar pain;
then a man will stand stock-still, hearing his youth
in the distant Latin chanting of a train.

Pray for us now. Grade 1 piano scales
console the lodger looking out across
a Midlands town. Then dusk, and someone calls
a child's name as though they named their loss.

Darkness outside. Inside, the radio's prayer –
Rockall. Malin. Dogger. Finisterre.

—Carol Ann Duffy, 'Prayer'

Preface

During the past decade or so I have become increasingly preoccupied with the idea of attempting a reinvention of religious thought as such. This is partly because it has become obvious that not one of the major religious traditions can survive in its present form. Not only have they all been stripped of their authority by philosophical and historical criticism (though of course they fail to recognize it), but because of the sweeping changes in philosophy since Kant and Hegel, they cannot be modernized. No proposed revision of any major religious tradition is likely to be able to satisfy *both* the present adherents *and* critical philosophers. Therefore, if despite the intellectual breakdown of all the existing traditions of religious thought we still consider religion important, we have to consider attempting a new beginning. This will not be easy, because most people still associate religion with belief in God and life after death—that is, with notions and aspirations that assert a spiritual realm both higher and more real than the world of sense. Today, however, we live in a purely human world, the world that our language gives us. It is all on one level, finite but unbounded, and it has no outside—and I am proposing to try to recreate religious thought for this new and only-human world! Inevitably, what I come up with is something very different from conventional ideas about "religion," and the few common elements are not immediately obvious. If in the end you reject my ideas but still want to be serious about religion, then the only option available to you is fundamentalism. Of course, if you would prefer to discard religion altogether, today's postmodern entertainment culture is the firmly established popular choice.

The second reason why I have felt attracted to the project of a large-scale reinvention of religious thought is that in 1998/1999 I found precisely such a reinvention already under way in ordinary language.[1] And although it may be a distinctly minority opinion, I still think that this discovery is very important. Plato made philosophy a pursuit for Supermen, master human beings, and so it remained up to Nietzsche and even beyond. I have reacted against this tradition by attempting to democratize philosophy, and have made the exhilarating discovery that the thinking of ordinary people is currently developing in close parallel with that of today's leading philosophers. Philosophy is democratizing *itself*. This has enabled me to say to my critics that my own thinking is not so wildly extreme and objectionable as they invariably claim. I could say to them, "I am not trying to foist *my own* ideas upon you; I am simply trying to show you what *you yourselves* have already begun to think."

So when in the ensuing first chapter I offer a very brief sketch of my progress thus far in the reinvention of religious thought, please do not forget my claim that this is *what you already think*, because much if not all of it is already incorporated into the idioms of your own everyday speech. As for the content of the re-invention, I repeat that we must entirely forget the old type of traditional organized religion, which involved a special alliance with a particular culture-area and language, a vast cosmic myth of Fall and Redemption, and a distinction between Heaven and earth. Instead, we will have to take up religion as "spirituality," a personal religious style. For in fact each of us needs to discover and express an appropriate response to the human situation, one through which we can become ourselves, make our own lives "meaningful" and offer a small but unique personal contribution to the overall value and beauty of the whole human life-world. In this way I find my own salvation whenever I do something, however small, to promote the salvation of others.

This general shift from organized religion to spirituality is summed up in the formula, "From *The World, the Soul, and God* to *Life and My Life*." Our world-view is postmodern and nihilistic: there is only the human life-world, a world made of language, a world without any absolute Beginning or End. In this transient scene each of us has a brief part to play—"my life"—and each of us needs to find a lifestyle through which to become oneself, and learn to do one's own thing in one's own way. By ardent world-love we can work out our own salvation, and at the same time make life more valuable for those who will succeed us.

For many if not most people today, the human life-world has no objective "meaning" nor "value" nor even reality apart from what human beings themselves put into it. Thus religion today is concerned not with finding redemption from sin, but with conquering nihilism. The way of life that does the trick is called solar living.[2] It is a synthesis of living and dying: we live expressively, by passing on and passing away all the time—committing ourselves to life so intensely that we conquer death by living a life that dies all the time.

Seen in this context, my small book called *The Way to Happiness* showed how the practice of "dying to the self" can help us to find great happiness in cosmic and selfless feeling. The present essay examines the part in our lives that may be played by various impossible loves, whether for non-existent objects, unavailable persons, or unattainable ideals.

Many thanks to Hugh Rayment-Pickard, who has once again made helpful criticisms of a late draft.

Don Cupitt
Cambridge
May 2006

So Far

I first began to read philosophy and religion intensively some fifty years ago. In those days it was still common for people to sum up their worldviews by referring to three different spheres, or kinds of entity: the World, the Soul, and God. *The world* was the whole created order of things visible and invisible as it had long been pictured in Christian theology, but with the proviso that in modern times "Creation" has been somewhat modified and secularized to become the Natural Order, the Universe as it is seen by modern science. *The soul* was the human self, a finite spiritual substance, centred, self-aware, morally responsible, naturally immortal, embodied in this life, and now actively relating itself to other selves, to the world, and above all to God. *God* was the god of the philosophers, the god of ethical monotheism, and the God believed in by Jews, Christians, and Muslims.

This basic world-picture, or way of representing the human situation, had been dominant in the West since antiquity. It had emerged, and then had become steadily clearer and more powerful, during the whole period between Plato and Augustine. Despite a long line of dissidents, it remained the scheme that most people worked with until about the time of Hegel, when it began to be replaced by a new and rather different scheme in which there are only two entities: *life* and *my life*.

In this new scheme, *life* is the whole historically-evolving human life-world, the world of constant human collaboration and exchange. This human world of ours is above all generated by and held within the flow of human language. The philosopher Ernest Gellner once said that before Kant human knowledge was some-

1

thing that emerged and took shape within a ready-made, rationally ordered world; but after Kant's revolution people began to see the world as taking shape within the sphere of human knowledge.[3] Our knowledge now comes first, and the world comes second. After Kant the great nineteenth-century thinkers increasingly place the emphasis not just on human knowledge, but upon the whole historical-cultural development of humanity. From Karl Marx onwards it slowly begins to be understood that everything is produced *within* the unfolding historical process, within the human life-world. The world of life, the world of language, is our milieu and is outsideless. Everything is immanent within the world, and the old habit of ultimately referring everything to an eternal realm beyond the world of human history is at an end. Metaphysics, or "God," is dead. There is only the world of "life," and within life there is *my life*, my span of life, my personal stake in the whole world of life, and the bit of it that I must claim as my own and do something with. In today's worldview *my life* has replaced *the soul*, while both *God* and *the world* have died and have been replaced by *life*. Augustine, Calvin and John Henry Newman all see *my soul*'s relation to *God* as the first and greatest topic of all; but in our new situation the first topic is the duty to assume personal responsibility for one's own life, to find one's own voice, and to make a personal contribution, however modest, to the whole evolving world of human life. Today, all Being is temporal, everything is held *within* the outsideless, flowing world of language, and the question of "the meaning of life" is up to you and up to me. It depends on our input. We all of us need to become ourselves and to do "our own thing" in our own way. If each of us can do just a little to enhance his or her own corner of the common life-world, the total value of life will be hugely enriched and religion will have done its job.

This new world-picture becomes more explicit in the thought of Heidegger and Wittgenstein, and clearer still in the philosophy of the last thirty years, as articulated by figures such as Gadamer, Habermas, Derrida, Rorty and Vattimo. But it has become completely clear to me only since I began to study the way it has become established within ordinary language since the Second World War. Now I say plainly that we will do best if we give up talking in terms of *the World*, *the Soul* and *God*, and instead talk simply in terms of *Life* and *my life*. Life is outsideless; it is all there is, and it is held within the continuing historical flow of human symbolic exchange, or "language." That is not the capital-T (or dogmatic) Truth, but it is the small-t (or pragmatic) truth, and as such it is all we have. It is only "weak" truth, but it is enough, so we should stick to it; and I am very impressed by the discovery that ordinary people have succeeded in reaching this position at about the same time as the leading philosophers.

The full implications of all this are only now becoming apparent. We are now talking about "radical humanism" in the sense that the human life-world really does come first and is outsideless, so that man really *is* "the measure of all things." But because we ourselves have access to ourselves and know ourselves only in and through our own language, we cannot claim any privileged position for ourselves: on the contrary, we too are each of us merely parts of the general flux. There is no extra-linguistic core-self, and hence the phrase "Empty radical humanism," using the word "Empty" in the Mahayana Buddhist sense. The human self is not a metaphysical substance, but merely one *persona* in the drama, one chain of steps in the general dance of everything. Like everything else, we are pouring out and passing away all the time; like everything else, we are made of words.

According to a popular saying, "What you see is what you get." All this flux of which we are only parts is outsidelessly all there is for us, and we can have no good reason for supposing that either sometime in the past or sometime hereafter, the human situation was or will again be radically better than it is now. No: all this, here and now, is all there is for us, and the triumph of the new outlook has coincided with the end of all versions of the beliefs in a lost Golden Age in the past, and a regained Golden Age, either here below or up above, at some time in the future. The sudden collapse of communist party government in many countries around 1989–1991 is a good marker of the moment when we suddenly lost the last great eschatology, and perhaps the last great Grand Narrative. From now on we give up the Grand-Narrative politics that tells a great world-story of how human beings long ago fell into captivity and now are slowly making their way towards their own future and final liberation. Instead we settle for the modest democratic sort of politics that can offer us no more than an End-less process of modest and piecemeal adjustment and reform. Correspondingly, in religion we quietly move out of the old kind of grand *organized religion*, with its very large-scale sacred cosmology and its Grand Narrative of Fall and Redemption, and we learn instead to work out a modest personal "spirituality" to live by.[4] We no longer live in the old way, suspended between corporate memory and corporate hope: we live simply in the present tense, and a *spirituality*, in the popular new sense of the word, is a personal religious lifestyle. For someone like me, who comes out of a Western Christian background, the appropriate spirituality for the new age will combine "solar" personal living with humanitarian social ethics. One can see such a spirituality already taking shape in the thought of people like Blake, Kierkegaard, Nietzsche and others (not that Nietzsche was any kind of humanitarian). It is a religious style that replaces the old spirituality of "the inner life" and of "saving one's soul" with a new spirituality that accepts our utter transience and has become radically extravertive. We live by self-expression, by pouring out and passing away; and I (in case you don't know) am a rather guttering candle that has about an inch left. When we are burnt out, we are over and done with; but in the meantime we should try to put on a good show. For achieving the goal of life, there will never be a better chance than we have now; so we had better burn fiercely *now*.

Such is the truth, for us, now. Everything else on the market—and there's plenty—is for people who cling to dead gods and are content to live in denial.

At the next stage in the argument, we now insist that the new worldview and spirituality are not Utopian. We are not free completely to remake the whole scheme of things, because a number of the traditional limits that circumscribe the human condition remain in place. I have, for example, been forcibly reminded of them by the way they keep surfacing in Derrida's great philosophy of language. In the traditional philosophical vocabulary they are temporality, contingency, and finitude—or in a more popular and reifying vocabulary: Time, Chance, and Death.[5]

We are always subject to *Time* because all our communicating, all our language, and all our understanding is always bit-by-bit, and strung out in time. Neither meaning nor truth can ever be communicated or comprehended all at once in a complete and simultaneous intuition. On the contrary, the sentence has not completely delivered its meaning until it has already slipped away into the past. We are always in arrears: even self-awareness is always in arrears, as is shown by the familiar example of the athlete who has already decided upon the correct stroke and has begun to execute it well *before* he has become conscious of the flight path of the ball coming towards him. Strange: consciousness does not govern our "mental" life, but is merely an after-effect of it.

From these and other very simple facts about what words are, and what sentences are, and how they move, much follows. We begin to see, for example, that the human self is not a privileged citadel, perspicuously self-aware and centred in itself, but merely something secondary and transient. Like everything else, and like all meaning and truth, the self is never delivered complete and simultaneous. There is no "real" meaning, and no absolute knowledge. On the contrary, in the case of whatever is said, the word order might have been different, the terms used might be different, and there will always be room for differences of interpretation. The new interpretation of the Death of God is the recognition that language is such, and works in such ways, that there cannot be a fixed Centre that anchors and sustains the whole world of language, holding all meaning steady and guaranteeing all truth. On the contrary, we are led irresistibly towards a new kind of linguistic phenomenalism—a new recognition of universal *contingency* and *finitude*. We are always subject to *Chance*, and *Death* is ubiquitous in the sense that everything is slipping and passing away all the time. All life is *dying* life, timebound, ambiguous, chancy, transient—and yet also, as I have always felt, heartbreakingly beautiful.

Criticizing Hegel, Kierkegaard was perhaps the first to show clearly that all our understanding is *retrospective*. Life is like rowing, where you sit looking backwards but have to move forwards, unable to see what you are heading towards: "Life can only be understood backwards; but it must be lived forwards." Here, Kierkegaard may be the first Western religious writer to give up the old idea that to live well we must live on the basis of clear and accurate knowledge—and, indeed, in the hope of *absolute* knowledge. On the contrary, he insists, we must live without any advance knowledge or metaphysical guarantees. We are like the man in the film who drives a lorry laden with explosives that may blow up at any moment, and will certainly blow up eventually. Or we are like rowers, unable to see where we are going, but compelled to row as fast as we can, despite the possibility that we may topple over a fall or hit a rock at any moment.

In this new post-metaphysical understanding of the human condition, faith is the courage to live hard in the face of our own clear recognition of the ambient limits of life—of its omnipresent temporality, contingency and finitude, of its continual slipping out of our grasp. Faith is no longer confidence in the reliability of something metaphysical or supernatural: faith is now the courage to *act*, to commit oneself to life, to live well and to enjoy life in the face of our modern awareness of life's utter contingency and transience.

Herein a very considerable religious shift has taken place. Since the first cities were established some six thousand years ago, nearly all religions have been much concerned with sustaining people's confidence that state society really can keep the terrors and uncertainties of life at bay. The annual cycle of seasons and feasts in the temple helped to both validate, and habituate people to, the annual round of agricultural tasks. The religions were great systems of mediation designed to protect ordinary people from too naked and unshielded a confrontation with the limits of life by projecting upon the Void whole worlds of stories, symbols, promises, and practices. They sought to create an impression of unlimited strength, security and permanence. But now in modern times the rise of natural science and science-based industrial society, and also of our new historical awareness, has brought about the collapse of the old systems of mediation and of supernatural belief. All of us, philosophers and ordinary people alike, have lost the old protective screen, and find ourselves confronting the unnerving challenges of life—its meaninglessness, its terrors and uncertainties—quite unshielded. And that is what I mean by "the return of the great questions": it is a time of spiritual crisis.

At the end of his life Heidegger felt stumped by this problem. He couldn't see a way out of the midnight-darkness that the human race had come to. We can only wait, he thought, and Samuel Beckett seemed to be of much the same mind. But, as I have argued for some years, there is a way of liberation, and it is by learning solar living. We must cast ourselves into, and identify ourselves entirely with, the continual passing-away that so terrifies us. "Green and dying," we must learn to live a dying life, and then we will find that "The more I give, the more I have."[6] The test will come on the day you are told that you are terminally ill and have only a few weeks or months of life left. If you can hear the news with equanimity, and thereafter continue to love life, living it to the full and pouring yourself out into it heedlessly until your last breath, then you are "solar," and have enacted in your own life the only conquest of death there is.[7]

In our world, the best way to live is by the practice of solar living. That is true, but it remains difficult to learn solar living, because we still cling to the idea that a bit of us remains outside time, and we are still a prey to the old anxieties and terrors that lead us to dream of entirely escaping from time and change. But one line of argument that we have already set out elsewhere runs as follows: if Time, Chance, and the threat of imminent Death fill us with overwhelming feelings of dread and horror, but yet cannot be escaped, there can be only one solution. Religion and culture must set about addressing those overwhelming feelings, and converting them into cosmic feeling. This is done by giving them a new interpretive framework, sublimating them, and revaluing them—an excellent example being the way in which the primitive biological terror and sense of vertigo that we naturally get when in a very high place can be converted by culture into a soaring cosmic feeling of release and spiritual exaltation. Similarly, religion has the power to revalue suffering so that we can learn to find joy in affliction; and religion can also help us to experience our own dying as mystical drowning in God or Nothingness. In these ways we can give up the mistaken attempt to *escape* from our fears, and learn instead how to go along with them, manage them, and transform them.[8]

To recapitulate, then: a great painted screen that was held up before our eyes used to protect us from too naked and terrifying an encounter with the truth about life. But recently the end of metaphysics and of supernatural belief has robbed us of that painted screen, leaving us exposed to a violent confrontation with our own deepest fears. In particular, the worst terror of all is the fear of the inner dissolution of one's own self, especially as a painful death approaches. At this point most people flee to cults, religious groups and the illusory security of Authority; but the solar person, amazingly, has found the trick of staying with that terror and making it the basis of a dying life. You actually live by pouring yourself out in self-expression and passing away all the time, so that living by losing oneself becomes a way of creatively affirming oneself *in passing.* Of course we do not ourselves *possess* the self we are all the time becoming, for we are *leaving it behind* all the time. To become solar is to become an expressive, creative person—but only at the price of continually moving on and leaving oneself behind. You truly become yourself only by losing yourself. One might call this "self-realization in retrospect."

Such is the first answer to the question of how on earth we are to learn and to practise the difficult art of solar living. The second line of answer, to be pursued in this book, arises from a study of the part played in our lives by what I call "impossible loves."

These impossible loves include, as we shall see, the dead, God, various unattainable or forbidden love-objects, and various impossible dreams or ideals. Between them, objects (or non-objects) in these four classes consume a surprising amount of our time and our emotional energy, especially as we grow older—that is, live past 70. At one level we are well aware that these heart's desires either don't exist, or can never be attained or realized: in short, we know that they are impossible loves. Nevertheless, we still cling obstinately to them, love them, aspire after them, and keep on thinking about them. We find that we can't let them go. They are extremely sweet to us, and they get sweeter and sweeter as the years pass. Usually bittersweet, I should add. But our impossible loves won't let us go. Are they utterly irrational, or do they have some religious significance for us? Perhaps in admitting their impossibility while still finding them very sweet, we are helping ourselves fully to see and accept life's limits, while yet loving life. In that case our impossible loves do have a function in teaching us how to be solar. They teach that it is possible to find a kind of sweetness in a state of Be-ing in which we simultaneously love something *and* know that we must continually let it go and let it go, again and again. There is a lyric sweetness in this pain of living all the time by loving and losing, loving and losing. And I am not ashamed to admit here that I find religious value and interest in the old pagan lyric poet's vision of the pain and the sweetness intrinsic to the transience of earthly beauty. It's only heightened by our modern realization that there is no *un*earthly beauty. *Earthly* beauty, transient though it is, is outsidelessly all there is for us. We have to make the most of it.

Love for the Dead

We humans are not eternal beings, inserted for a short probationary period into this temporal world, and then withdrawn from it. No, Wordsworth was wrong—on this point at least. We didn't come here from Elsewhere: we arose here. We are through-and-through temporal beings, and we cannot begin to imagine what *extra*-temporal personal life, relationships, thinking, action, and language could be. We simply *are* our own lives in time: in time we first arose, and in time we will come to an end. Every one of us will die in due course, and death is simply the cessation of life. As the stock phrase has it, **When you're dead, you're dead**. You are no more. You will be survived by various remains of you—your body, your possessions, the various traces of your work and activities, people's memories of you, and so on—but you the participant social person will no longer exist. By that I do not mean that some vital bit of you that used to be in your body has now left your body and gone elsewhere. I mean only that your life has ended. You are no longer **in the loop** or **on the scene;** you are no longer taking an active part in the day-to-day exchanges that are the stuff of life. You are no longer **in the swim**, a phrase that invokes the familiar image of temporal life in general as a great river in which we contemporaries are all floating downstream together.

It is impossible to exaggerate how profoundly we are embedded or immersed in time. We are not timeless substances that just happen to be living lives in time for a while; no, we simply *are* our own lives, and they are parts of a certain stretch of human history. We are assembled, we come together and are born in time, and we will in due course dissolve in time. All talk of *coming into the world* or *passing away* is misleading if it implies that we were put together somewhere else and then dispatched into this world, and that when we die we depart and journey away to some other realm. There is only this world, the world of our life, and it is outsideless. Nothing comes "into" it or journeys "out" of it. It is finite but unbounded, and there are no secret doorways giving access to other worlds. *All this* is all there is for us.

From all of this it is—or should be—quite clear that my death is not an event in my life, nor it is in any way a threshold or boundary the like of which all of us will one day have to cross. It is true of course that we can and do make arrangements for the disposition of our property and the care of our dependents after our own lives have ended; and it is also true that many or most people very much hope to be remembered. One may wish to think of being remembered as a sort of objective immortality, and undoubtedly some very talented people do have an intense longing for posthumous fame. But the more we think about it, the more clearly we understand that there is no meaning at all in the suggestion that Don Cupitt, 1934–2014 or so, who was a human life lived, a datable, locatable chain of events and activities within history, could somehow be plucked out of his own context and given a second span of life in some other world. It's a fantasy. It makes no sense because I am part of my context in life, thoroughly interwoven and continuous with it. "I" cannot be removed from my setting in life. I *am* the time of my life, and if I've got any sense I'll try to make sure that I *have* **the time of my life**—that is, live my life to the full while it lasts.

There is, then, no "life after death" in the popular sense, and at a certain level everybody knows it. And yet . . . and yet as our lives pass we cannot help but become aware of the extent to which we continue to yearn after and pursue various impossible objects, loves, dreams, and projects. Why do we do this—and indeed, do it more and more? What is the role of these "impossible loves" in our lives, and especially in our spiritual lives?

Of these impossible loves, love for the dead is an excellent example to begin with, because even after we have become quite sure that our dead are simply non-existent, we cannot help noticing that we go on loving them more and more. Enthroned in our imaginations as venerated ancestors, benign and unchanging, they seem to become ever more real and significant. Even if in life we were often in conflict with them, in death they are "at peace," beyond conflict, and very dear to us. They are reference-points. We think of them daily, and somehow cannot help imagining that our thinking of them is a form of *communing* with them, and that it is a very good thing to be doing.

I confess *I* do this. And because I have striven so hard for a completely demythologized and illusion-free philosophical and religious outlook, it presents me with an acute difficulty. The dead are dead: they no longer exist, and we can do nothing for them. Even Jesus (ever the impatient young man) says, "Leave them! Leave the dead to bury their dead." So why am I addicted to a sort of ancestor-cult? To be solar is to be wholly committed to the life that one is actually living now. Why do I want to spend time every day in useless daydreaming, hankering after non-existent beings? Am I already beginning to think of **joining the majority** sometime in the next twenty years or so, and becoming another such being *myself*?

That use of "the majority" to mean "the dead" reminds us of yet another illusion: that "the dead" are somehow *together* in one place. Of course they are not. When a spouse dies, the survivor may speak of looking forward to following his or her partner so that the two can be "reunited" in heaven, in death, or in the grave; but it's all an illusion. For the survivor death is an "eternal" separation that does not admit of any reunion at all. The dead person has not gone anywhere, and it is not waiting to be joined. He or she has simply ceased to be, and is not anywhere.

Sometimes we feel inclined to follow the ancients, and see the condition of the dead as *pitiable*. But the dead are nowhere and are not in any condition, so that from a strictly rational point of view they are neither pitiable nor enviable. It follows that some*one* who desires death is not desiring some*thing*: he simply wishes to cease living because his life has become intolerable to him.

The point at issue here was discussed recently by the Oxford philosopher Bede Rundle in his book on the great cosmological question of *Why there is Something rather than Nothing.*[9] We are always inclined to reify Nothing, rather as we do when we fancy that an Unidentified Flying Object must be a real and rather special object, perhaps extra-terrestrial or supernatural. But in fact, *there being Nothing* is not in itself another possible state of affairs that can be set alongside and compared with *there being Something*. So the question, *Why is there Something rather than Noth-*

ing? amounts to no more than the question *Why is there Some-thing?*, which in turn invites the positivist retort, *Whyever not?*

Just as *there being Nothing* is not a real state of affairs whose probability can be estimated and compared with the probability of the alternative state of affairs that is *there being Something*, so the dead are not a class of beings who are in a certain condition and can be compared with the living. **They are history**, as the phrase goes. They are in the past.

The more I think of it the more I see that the dead, and in particular my own dead, are impossible objects of love. And if love for the dead is indeed an impossible love, why do I seem to spend some time on it every day? Why can't I just forget the dead?

Here is the first hint of the answer. If love for someone who is dead is love for an impossible object that is not in any condition and is not in any sense *there*, then it must be a particularly gra-tuitous, unrewarded, and therefore unselfish kind of love. Could the practise of love for one's dead perhaps be seen as training in objectless, unrewarded, purely generous love—like the Mahayana Buddhist's *metta* (universal compassion) and the Christian's pure *agapé?*

To say this is to offer an hyper-Kierkegaardian suggestion. Ki-erkegaard himself, in his discussion of love for one who is dead,[10] does not say that such a love is in any sense impossible. For him, it seems, the dead are in a condition: they are *in God*, or *in eternity*. Love for them is unselfish because being in eternity, they are in no position to respond to our love. They do not show pleasure, and they do not reply. But those who interpret Kierkegaard realisti-cally will say that for him faith enables a real communion with the dead, whereas my post-Derridean account of the human condition renders many of our most cherished affections impossible and absurd. Nevertheless, we cling to them, and the absurd impossibil-ity of our action reveals our condition to us. It provides a kind of religious education. It makes *us* what we are, and *love* what it is: absurd, objectless love is "divine" love. The whole *point* of "loving God" is that it is loving something that doesn't exist.

I can't bear to stay at that level—at least, not this early in the book—nor perhaps can you. It hurts too much. Let us descend for a while, and ask: Who exactly *are* "our dead"? Principally, they are those with whom we stand in a parent-child relationship—that being the deepest and most constitutive relationship of all. Only in the very rare case of a "great love" does the man-woman relation-ship rise to the same level—a level few dare claim to have reached.

I cannot forbear to add here a mention of those of your and my children who didn't quite make it, such as the few grams of tissue that aborted spontaneously—or "miscarried"—at three months in April 1964, some fourteen weeks after my marriage. As people say, **You never forget the one you lost**, especially if it was the very first. And I mention this case of the child that **never made it** as a particularly clear example of an "impossible" life-long love that one can never forget, a love so irrational and absurd that it seems to be divine.

In any case, the chief place amongst our dead belongs to those whose child or parent we are. After them come a few other very close relations—a spouse, a sibling, a few mentors. And for the individual that seems to be all. Communal memorials take many different forms around the world: the finest and most moving I ever saw was the little clan shrine that occupied a focal position in an old Chinese walled village. Kat Hing Wai, in the Mainland territory of Hong Kong, was built in the sixteenth century by a clan named Tang. Some fifty years ago it got its great bronze doors back, and because of the catastrophic destruction of the country's architectural heritage in recent years, it is one of the best things of its kind remaining in the whole of China. A high stone wall surrounds the tiny village. Inside is a short main street with many little alleyways, along which one-storey houses are packed very close. The stream over which the village is built has been divided into parallel watercourses by which each household is supplied. As members of a single clan, the villagers need to know their exact relationship to everyone else. The clan shrine is a small and dimly-lit room where oil lamps illuminate a few small offerings and walls covered with yellowing photographs and inscriptions commemorating *all* the community's dead. Each day, people call informally at the clan shrine and, as it were, refresh their relationship with their dead. And as people do in many parts of the world, they talk to their dead.

At Ixtassou in the *pays Basque* there survives a strikingly similar example from within Latin Christianity. A covered way surrounds the whitewashed exterior wall of the church, and each family has perhaps a meter of the wall, to which are affixed small plaques commemorating deceased members. Here as in China living family members can and do pay regular visits to their dead, sometimes leaving flowers.

In earliest Latin Christianity, believers wished to maintain communion with the dead martyrs whose relics they had preserved, at first in catacombs. One way of doing this was to celebrate the Eucharist on the anniversary of the martyrdom, down below ground in the very presence of the relics. The word *refrigerium* (refreshment) was used in connexion with this special use of the Mass for communicating with the venerated dead.

Later, in seventeenth-century Rome sharp controversies arose over Matteo Ricci's proposal that the Chinese way of venerating the dead should be allowed to continue within the practice of Chinese Catholic Christianity. Eventually Clement XI decided the matter in the negative in 1704 and 1715: the Catholic cult of saints and their relics was laudable and Christian, whereas the Chinese way of maintaining communion with dead family members was deeply objectionable. In retrospect, one wonders why. The desire to commemorate one's dead is felt in much the same way by people all around the world, and it finds expression in many exotic practices. Everywhere it is irrational and absurd: it shows human beings attempting the impossible, trying somehow to overcome the eternal separation that is death. It is utterly futile, and all the religious beliefs about "life after death" are absurd. But the very fact that our love for the dead cannot be stifled even by the knowledge of its impossibility and absurdity makes it somehow divine. This excessive, objectless, irrepressible love for the dead is *divine* love. Being human and therefore speakers, we can recognize that some things are quite impossible, and that contingent possibilities are continually being left unfulfilled, and soon lost forever. Contingency, finitude, sadness, yearning, and cosmic love are all tangled together in a single package. **That's life**. It is bitterbittersweet.

two

3

Great Love, and Eternal Separation

T
wo very different forms of heterosexual 'great' love have each been thought of as aiming to transcend, or at least to challenge, the ordinary limits of life.

The first is the Romantic *grande passion* of those who are so swept by passion and so exclusively and intensely fixated upon the Other that they forget all else, including even their own selfhood. Thus Catherine Earnshaw[11] and Heathcliff each wish to *become* the other, speaking of the other as 'my life', or 'my soul' (though it is notable that Heathcliff does not in the very same words reciprocate Catherine's statement that 'I *am* Heathcliff'). Their passion is reckless and imprudent; **it stops at nothing**, driving relentlessly towards madness or death. In fact, almost inevitably such impetuosity ends in the latter—no doubt because a double death or *Lovers' Leap* from the local cliff traditionally used for that purpose is the only artistically satisfactory conclusion that such a story as theirs can reach. In myth and folktale, in fiction and in opera, great love customarily ends in tragedy. In real life—if I may be permitted that expression—a *grande passion* is more likely to be viewed as a crazy obsession, and to end with a conviction for 'stalking' and a court order. The very idea of a reciprocated *grande passion* settling down into a peaceful marriage seems somehow incongruous.

In antiquity generally, and among sober people of the world in all ages, intense romantic love has been regarded as a tragic affliction or as madness—a state of possession by a mischievous god. To be sure, folklore, ballads, and other romantic literature regarded the *grande passion* with much more sympathy, and it has always been a very popular subject in the opera house and the theatre. But even in the Romantic era it was hard to envy those in its grip, and even harder to admire their actions. The violent emotion that grips them has the effect of making them appear to be self-centered or even solipsistic. They talk only about themselves and the torments they are suffering. Catherine can go on for a long time about the extreme violence of her feeling for Heathcliff, but she doesn't seem to perceive him clearly at all. (Nor do we, in fact.) A love as blind as *that* almost ceases to be love at all, as if Heathcliff is in the end not really much more than a convenient peg for Catherine's death-wish. We should prefer the sharp sparring of Beatrice and Benedict, or the cozy bickering of the long-married. At least they see each other's weaknesses clearly.

I do not, however, conclude that the impossible yearnings of a person in the grip of a *grande passion* are in *no* sense religiously instructive. On the contrary, when excessive Romantic love becomes self-destructive it is very like religious enthusiasm run amok. Such frantic excitability in early Christianity drove people to court martyrdom, or to fast almost unto death; and the best religious authorities have always discouraged it. Nonetheless, it has often cropped up, and is still encountered today. To avoid becoming sidetracked on the subject of suicide bombers, I recall instead the occasion many years ago when somebody came to talk to me about his own intense religious desire to perform a public suicide by fire. This was not long after the Jan Palach incident in Czechoslovakia; but in my friend's case I could not help noticing that he spoke much more clearly and eloquently about the intensity of his yearning for death by fire than about *what* great Cause his self-immolation would serve, or *how* he thought the act might help the Cause along. He was like a person in the grip of an extreme lust, one who is so intoxicated by his fixation that he does not see its hapless object clearly as a person at all. So I did what I could to talk my visitor out of an obsession that I couldn't see as being religiously or morally fruitful.

With that I set aside the *grande passion* as a topic, and turn instead to the claim that something "eternal" can be discovered in the peaceful daily routines of a long marriage. In our own time this claim is symbolized by the practice of giving an "eternity ring"—one appropriately set with an unbroken circle of gemstones. Two vivid examples of the claim are very early, dating from about CE 1420, and appear in English funerary monuments that are worth describing in detail.

At Strelley, to the east-northeast of Nottingham, England, a tomb chest stands in the center of the chancel of the parish church, and on it lie life-size effigies in Chellaston alabaster of Sir Sampson de Strelley and his lady.[12] What is remarkable is that their right hands are joined. Since they presented their village with such a handsome church, we must assume that the Strelleys were devout, but in the Christian tradition marriage is only a temporary relationship that is terminated by death. A dead couple are then correctly represented in attitudes of prayer and with eyes closed, prepared for their *separate* appearances on the Day of Judgment. But the Strelleys presumably wished to assert that their marriage would continue beyond death, an interpretation confirmed by the even clearer example of the Greenes of Drayton House, in Lowick church, Northamptonshire, England.[13] In this case the contract of 1415 for the monument still survives. It obliges the 'kervers of Chellaston' (that is, alabaster) to supply images in which husband and wife hold hands, and it was signed when both were living. The two slightly quaint but very charming figures are wide-eyed and appear very much alive. Lady Greene smiles demurely. Sir Ralph Greene looks manly. What the Greenes want us to remember about them is *not* the pious spirit in which, after being parted by death, they each went their separate ways to Judgment; rather they proclaim that they deeply loved each other in life, and that for them this purely human love of theirs was as "sacred" and "eternal" as anything in the Church's sacred world of revealed truth. Yes, ordinary married love can be eternal love.

The Greenes and the Strelleys stand in a long tradition of lay protest. The Latin Christianity of the Middle Ages remained a basically celibate religion, whose doctrine, rituals and institutions were heavily skewed towards teaching the all-round superiority of the Sacred realm inhabited by the élite celibate church-within-the-church, which then (as now) was a corporation of religious and secular clergy and nuns. The result was a culture in which the whole lay experience of life, including sexual, domestic, and family activities, was devalued. The lay protest against all this was led by the poets, and it eventually secured a (partial) victory in the Reformation and in the Catholic Counter-Reformation.

The protest is entirely understandable. But is it an "impossible" one? How can it be claimed that there is something "eternal" in marriage, when the parties themselves pledged themselves to each other only "till death do us part"? Don't we all know that every

marriage, including the most secure and unbreakable, must in fact
end in eternal separation?

I have two counter-arguments. The first is that our thinking
about marriage and domestic life should not be unduly dominated
by the linear view of time as relentlessly ticking away and moving
towards its inevitable end, for marriage and domestic life are not
"historical," but exist in mythic, "golden" time. And the second
argument is that what makes marriage seem "theological" is the
fact that its essential nature is so hidden and deeply buried, so
private, that even the parties themselves don't know what its truth
is. Hence the perception of it as being quasi-sacred.

Just because marriage is so private and hidden, we lack public examples of it. No major novel depicts a "great" marriage, or
could do so, but Tolstoy's novella *Happy Ever After* can be cited as
a superb study of a marriage beginning to go wrong. The general
difficulty is that there is no point of view from which the truth
about a marriage can be observed. The parties cannot claim
absolute knowledge of each other, and there is no space for a third
party. Yet interestingly, it is this very inaccessibility of the truth
about marriage that makes it so religiously peaceful as a couple
gradually become content to let more and more become tacit.
They don't *have* to be neurotically articulate, but can be content to
leave many, many things unsaid. Eventually they create a large and
growing area of tacit mutual understanding and trust that opens
onto the vast peaceful space of domestic life.

If these ideas seem obscure, perhaps I may with permission
cite the only readily accessible example. My wife and I have lived
in the same house for a little over 40 years, during which time,
people say, "Nothing has changed." Time seems to move in circles
and to keep renewing itself, as another day or week or year or generation comes round. Cots and high chairs returned recently after
a thirty-year absence. What we are to do is debated by reference
to what we have "always" done, and no doubt "always" will do. The
"always" here, as in the common expression "He always used to
say, . . ." signifies that we see domestic life *not* as a chain of unique
events in linear time building towards a grand conclusion, but in
terms of repetition and cyclical recurrence. The domestic year in
that respect resembles the liturgical year of religion: it doesn't get
anywhere, and isn't *meant* to get anywhere. It is content with its
own eternal return. Sometimes its routine is disrupted by periods
of absence, illness or hospitalization; but when this happens there

is a tacit agreement that **life must go on,** and we will of course restore normality as soon as we possibly can. And so we do.

I have avoided talking about married love as an alleged lifelong erotic passion pledged to remain fixated upon a single object and refusing ever to allow itself to be displaced. This view of marriage concentrates attention upon a kind of unconditional commitment and a quest for absolute security "for ever," which is made impossible by the contingency of life and the knowledge that every marriage, including even the best of all, must end in an eternal and inconsolable separation. Instead, I have suggested that we can see the religious significance of marriage if we see it in the classical protestant way as creating a sort of miniature monastery—a private or even "sacred" haven of refuge from the tyranny of linear time, competition, and death that reigns in the public or "historical" world. We can scrap the deeply wrong and anxiety-inducing idea that life ought to be spent in preparing for death, and instead enjoy the daily, weekly, yearly, and generational return of the same domestic routines. I hold my child—and then, a bit later, hold my grandchild. So the wheel turns, and I forget about death. **Life goes on**.

But the whole thing depends upon mutual trust and a talent for leaving more and more unsaid. Marriage, too, has to become solar: we live by letting go and regaining, letting go and regaining, over and over, until the time comes for the final letting go. Which must be done without regret.

Love for a Dead God

After someone who has been very close to us dies, it can often happen that in a moment's forgetfulness we find ourselves turning to them and even speaking to them—until with a sharp pang of grief we realize our error. Wordsworth describes a mistake of this kind made in the year 1813, when he experienced and sought to share one of his sudden moments of joy in nature:

> Surprized by joy—impatient as the Wind
> I wished to share the transport—Oh! With whom
> But Thee, long buried in the silent Tomb,
> That spot which no vicissitude can find?
> Love, faithful love recalled thee to my mind—
> But how could I forget thee![14]

In the remainder of this sonnet Wordsworth recalls his missing companion's death the year before, and his realization then that he was now eternally separated from her:

> I stood forlorn,
> Knowing my heart's best treasure was no more;
> That neither present time nor years unborn
> Could to my sight that heavenly face restore.

The loss he is talking about is that of his daughter Catherine, born in 1808, who had died in June 1812 at the age of about three-and-a-half. Her mischievousness and vitality had deeply affected him, because she helped him to recapture some of his own child-hood joy in life. Now she was dead and gone eternally—but he could not outgrow his intense love for her. Hence the double irony that the poem is addressed to her as if she were still alive, even though it springs from the heart-wrenching mistake of having for a moment spoken to her as if she were not dead. The poem can't help reprising the error that it was inspired by—and such is the paradox and the painfulness of an impossible love. Catherine was no more, but Wordsworth couldn't stop loving her and speaking to her.

Later in the nineteenth century many of the same griefs, discomforts, and paradoxes were repeated as great numbers of people experienced in their own lives the Death of God. If all your life you have been in the habit of praying, it is not at all easy to give up prayer merely because you have lost faith in God. Some people continued to pray, but used a demythologized kind of prayer, as in the oft-quoted maxim: "Who rises from his knees a better man, his prayer is granted." For such people prayer was a way of examining one's conscience and making good resolutions. The socialist Beatrice Webb describes in her autobiography *My Apprenticeship* how she came gradually to sum up the two great commandments—that we must love God, and that we must love our neighbour—in the second, because neighbour-love was traditionally the great test of our love for God. Since she needed to continue praying, prayer became for her a way of cultivating a quasi-divine Love for one's fellow humans, and dedicating oneself to their service. In like manner others gradually turned prayer into meditation, of which not very much had previously been heard in the Protestant world. The religious traditions of South and East Asia began to supply the West with a great variety of new styles and techniques of meditation, and they continue to do so to this day.

After their loss of belief in God, many people not only wanted to continue praying, but also wanted to go on expressing many of the old feelings towards God and to continue participating in the traditional theological practices and arguments. Worship was very often displaced, first onto the Whole, and then perhaps onto Nature—either of which substitutions was easy enough. It was much harder to find someone other than God to take all the blame traditionally heaped upon God, and often people found themselves attacking the non-existent God: "The only excuse for God is that he does not exist." Here the great difficulty is that people really do need to voice their complaints. They want to articulate their sense of life's unfairness and general unsatisfactoriness. Why all the hard cases; why so much less good than we were led to expect? Hitherto, belief in God had provided an excellent vocabulary with which to voice one's complaint and to consider various standard counter-arguments: it is better for us to have freewill even if we make some very costly mistakes; it is better for us to have a law-governed natural world, even if the operation of the laws sometimes causes much suffering, and so on. But lacking any God to struggle with and about, how are we to conduct these existentially vital arguments? Human beings want to find contentment in life: they want to discover, understand, and accept a larger scheme of things—and to see how their own lives fit into it. But the Death of God seems to deprive the individual of the only really good vocabulary for debating these matters.

Hence the "impossible" paradox that the Death of God makes people acutely and belatedly aware that theological arguments really were about matters of great importance to us all. The Death of God left generations of people filled with an aching nostalgia not only for the dead God, but also for *theology*.

Of all English writers, Thomas Hardy best reflects these puzzling difficulties. (In this he may be seen to resemble the American author, Mark Twain.) Hardy was, of course, not only a great novelist and poet; he was also an ecclesiastical architect and designer, whose work survives in many Dorset churches. He had a considerable knowledge of and love for the old village Anglicanism of the pre-Victorian era in which he preferred to set his novels. He was much more than "the village atheist, brooding over the village idiot." At Christmas-time his poetry still finds him "hoping it might be so," and he rather enjoys the paradox of continuing to argue with the dead God. His poem "A Plaint to Man," dated 1909–1910 and first published in the collection *Satires of Circumstance* (1914), ratchets up the paradoxes particularly tightly.[15] Here the God who does not exist does all the talking: he asks Man, Why did you invent me? When you first crawled up "out of shapeless slime" why "did there come to you / The unhappy need of creating me/—a form like your own—for praying to?" My various qualities came only from you, and only by you were projected out in front of your own eyes:

> My virtue, power, utility,
> Within my maker must all abide,
> Since none in myself can ever be,
>
> One thin as a phasm on a lantern-slide
> Shown forth in the dark upon some dim sheet,
> And by none but its showman vivified.

But now, continues God, "I dwindle by the day" and you have
been locked into your consoling but also disabling error for so
long that you are ill-prepared for life without me,

> . . . with dependence placed
> On the human heart's resource alone,
> In brotherhood bonded close and graced.

The God that Hardy talks about is the God of the ordinary
Christian believer, the God of what Derrida calls "restricted
theology."[16] This is the God of religious faith: a heavenly Father, a
moral providence, and the one to whom believers pray in church
and at home; the God revealed in Jesus Christ, who guarantees
that whatever the appearances to the contrary may be in the short
term, nevertheless in the long term good will prevail and all will
be well. But behind the hard-working God of personal everyday
religion is a broader "general theology" in which God is the ultimate founder, orderer and upholder of everything, and especially
of all reality, intelligibility, truth and value. Apart from the rather
thin tradition of scepticism, the main body of Western thought
has been completely dominated by this general theology, and it
was only with Nietzsche that a serious attempt to diagnose it and
root it out at last began. But both Nietzsche and more recently
Derrida have suspected that general theology is so written into
the structure of our language that it controls the way we think. It
decides the very nature of reason and valid argument—in which
case we may *never* be able entirely to shake it off. Perhaps the best
we can do is keep on trying to expose and undermine it, a process
Derrida called "deconstruction."

Two interesting and powerful metaphors help to explain the
point here. First, consider the generality of signs and words. A
common noun is not a specific label that can be stuck to one thing
only: it can be applied to any of the indefinitely large number
of things that fall under its "intension" or "connotation." It may
invoke any of and all of the members of a whole class: it calls up,
unifies, and activates an entire domain. Hence Derrida's oft-quoted dictum: "The sign and divinity have the same place and time of
birth. The age of the sign is essentially theological."[17] The power of
the sign is the power of God.

The second metaphor is that of absolute monarchy, where a
complex domain is seen as unified and grounded in a central image. On a cycle wheel, each bit of the rim is directly and equally
related to the central hub, and that "monarch" is the centre from

which all authority and organizing power radiate outwards. So, along with patriarchy in family relationships, kingship has been an immensely potent model for thought about society. It shows us how all the constituents of a complex domain can be united and made into a coherent and powerful body by their common relationship to a central founding and governing author/authority.

Against this background, we can now raise a number of questions. What gives to words their power over things: how is language able to summon up and order a world? What has given to the fleeting world of Becoming such reality and order as it has? How is objective truth possible, and how is objective value possible? Now we begin to see how deeply the idea of God is embedded in Western thought—further back indeed than religion, for God is everywhere presupposed as the founding, controlling, empowering Centre or Ground that underpins everything, securing its stability and its objectivity, and making it intelligible to us whom he has made in his own image. We think and speak only *after* God, in the sense that, such as it is, our understanding and control of the world entirely depends upon his. It is not surprising that to a traditional metaphysical theist (and realist) anyone who ceases to believe in the objective existence of God must be immediately plunged into a crisis of Nihilism. His whole world must become a howling, unintelligible chaos of transient fragments; and he is bound to think that his very sanity is radically threatened. Hence the curious fact about strong pre-critical religious believers that everyone must have noticed: they always consider themselves to be alone in the light, and feel quite sure that everyone outside their own circle is dwelling in a chaos of spiritual, moral, and intellectual darkness.

They have everything. They have objective reality; an objective, intelligible, ready-made order of things out there; objective Truth all around; words with their true meanings eternally grounded in the divine Mind; a sure knowledge of right and wrong; a hotline to the eternal One; and complete assurance that their own eternal salvation is guaranteed by him. All this is hidden from the wise, and has been revealed to mere babes. It gives them the confidence to look down upon modern science, and airily to dismiss the central ideas of modern biology. They know better, *far* better.

Thus one may say that a conservative believer in God inherits a colorful popular version of the leading axioms of Western thought. From Augustine to Calvin, and from Descartes to Husserl, Western thinkers always rated intuitive or immediate understanding above discursive or mediated understanding. The contrast is indeed written into the New Testament:

> For now we see in a [sc. polished bronze] mirror dimly, but then face to face. Now I know in part; then I shall understand fully, even as I have been fully understood.[18]

The ideal after which philosopher and saint alike aspire is that of visionary, total, immediate understanding and mastery. It involves a perfect and perspicuous self-possession and self-knowledge. It involves absolute knowledge of the essence of the object known; and, so far as our thinking and our active life in the world are seen to depend upon language, it involves the belief that we can achieve complete mastery of language. As we speak, we can be so completely in control of what we mean by what we say, that our language is in effect completely transparent: it in no way obstructs, but instead simply opens up to us an immediate grasp and control of the real world out there.

This complex of ideas is particularly vivid in the leading figures of the Western religious tradition (Paul, Augustine, Calvin, J.H. Newman . . .); in the leading "I-philosophers" (including especially Descartes, Husserl and the French phenomenologists); and in a great number of the most confident and vociferous propagandists for natural science. To this day it remains strong—witness the fact that the world's leader in scientific achievement is also its bastion of Evangelical Protestantism. The common *philosophical* ground of these two great cultural forces is *realism*: a belief in the objective reality of the world and of God, who, because he *is* the absolute embodiment of all these ideas, is the One after whom every serious-minded Westerner aspires. When we say that God is our Origin and our End, we mean that his reality, establishing everything, launches us upon a lifelong quest of which he is necessarily himself the Goal.

That's the God that was; and the most interesting and important philosophies of the past 330 years have in various ways been attempts to overthrow or to undermine and escape from this whole scheme of thought. It has proved to be an extraordinarily difficult enterprise, the main landmarks of which have been the principal writings of Hume, Kant, Nietzsche, Heidegger and Derrida. In Derrida's case, future historians of philosophy will doubtless give most prominence to the year 1967, when he published *Of Grammatology*, *Writing and Difference*, and *Speech and Phenomena*, a collection of closely-related essays about Husserl. Easily the best of his works, these set forth in his typically modest, veiled, and riddling way, the most thorough and comprehensive exposure and undermining of the main axioms of Western thought that anyone has yet achieved.

Derrida's methods are complex and controversial, but his central argument seeks to demonstrate the impossibility of the completely "present," pure, and unmediated visionary grasp of reality that we have ascribed to God and have dreamed of acquiring for ourselves. It is ruled out by the nature of language, which always creates and delivers meaning by a complicated process of foregrounding what it takes to be primary, clear, and straight, while at the same time repressing or deferring what it takes to be secondary and relatively dark and indirect. Thus, as in psychoanalysis, there is always a subtext: something that has been deliberately left unsaid, but which nevertheless is sure to find ways of "resurfacing" and making itself felt.

I am suggesting here that one very short and simple way to explain what Derrida is doing is to note that he was prompted by the French psychoanalyst Jacques Lacan to read the whole of psychoanalytical theory as a set of doctrines that describe not the workings of our "minds"—whatever *they* are—but rather how *language* works. And the upshot is that we must finally give up all metaphysical dreams of attaining pure self-possession, visionary knowledge, and complete control of reality. Instead, we must accept that language itself commits us irrevocably to time, secondariness, and ambivalence, in a realm that has no outside. As Richard Rorty puts it, "interpretation goes all the way down." Pure truth, pure and unmediated contact with Reality, is never reached. There cannot be a final disclosure of the Real at the end of time. On the contrary, as long as there are human beings who talk about such things, truth will continue to be exactly what it is now: the current state of the argument—no more and no less.

His 1967 books won Derrida his place in the canon of Western thinkers, but he admitted even then that the doctrines he was trying to subvert may be ineradicable. In this still largely Hegelian age, the difficulty is that any rational arguments you try to mobilize against Reason have already been anticipated by it. So it always engulfs you, and you lose. As Derrida shows, the deep assumptions of Western thought that Plato and others laid down so powerfully control our ideas about reality, meaning, truth and so on, that we cannot find arguments *against* them that do not already *presuppose* them. It follows that, as in the case of Hegel the System always wins, so in the present case God always wins. We cannot bring him down by rational argument, because he alone determines what is to *count* as rational argument. Having comprehensive control of the agenda, he cannot be challenged directly. Our best hope is that by using Derrida's indirect method of deconstruction we can make God seem to wobble briefly—but He'll be back.

This leads us to suppose that if Derrida is right, his work shows that Western philosophy has reached the limit of its possible development and can go no further. This uneasy suspicion is strengthened by the well-known fact that although by 1967 Derrida had pushed "the Death of God" further than anyone previously, he himself remained oddly haunted by the ghost of God for the rest of his life. He still hankered after the God whom he had shown to be impossible.

This highly simplified exposition of mine strongly suggests that however successfully you *dis*prove God, God always seems to return at a deeper level. Having used philosophy to show that the anthropomorphic God of popular religion cannot exist, we move to a deeper level and clutch to ourselves the God of classical philosophical theism. Then if we demolish metaphysics and show that the sublime God of the philosophers cannot exist either, we move to a yet deeper level and equate God with a primal *Ur-Ground* prior to any specific way of constituting philosophy. And perhaps even before the *Ur-Ground*, there is the *Ein Sof* of the Kabbala, which is yet more dark and remote. So every dissolution of God at one level simply pushes him down to a deeper and more general level; and the harder we battle to free ourselves *from* God, the further we go in the great classical spiritual journey into the divine Darkness and Nothingness. The modern professional atheist is merely a monk *manqué* who has absent-mindedly forgotten what he wants and where he is going.

Derrida does not fail to note a second and likewise dark return of God. I have in mind a place or an occasion from which God is *conspicuously absent*. The phrase seems to be an oxymoron, but we have all heard a professed atheist describe a very dreary place as "godforsaken." Some towns—I refrain from citing examples— are so completely lacking in merit, in attractiveness, in interest that . . . that what? Surely, the use of the word "godforsaken" presupposes the old outlook, in which people saw God as the only Ground of the world's intelligibility, goodness, beauty, interestingness—and so axiomatically that if God were removed, the world could not be anything more than a blank, featureless, dreary desert. In that case, surely no atheist can self-consistently describe a place as being "godforsaken." But he does: people whose outlook is quite post-religious *do* still use words like "godforsaken" and "soulless." How then can the words be used meaningfully? I suggest that we are now at last building a world from which God is totally absent, and in this final forgetting of God it can still happen that God's utter absence becomes *conspicuous*.[19] It isn't merely that God's absence is to be attributed to certain people's absent-mindedness or forgetfulness. No, it is rather that the place is so utterly derelict that we cannot help suspecting that God himself has left it blighted by his abandonment and discarding of it.

I suspect then that our newest and most atheistic visions of the world will for some time retain vestiges of the older theistic world-view. The world *after* God will go on being haunted by the ghost *of* God, much as the self-styled unbeliever admits by his very use of the term "atheist" that God was there before him. The relativistic world in which everything is secondary will continue—perhaps, as Derrida suspects, forever?—to presuppose a world in which God and all the "absolutes" that he has established come first. The godforsaken world will continue to presuppose the God-created world, and the unbeliever will—perhaps forever—continue to come in second, *after* the believer.

Notice in the previous paragraph the use of the words *relativistic* and secondary. They signal a presupposed difference between the absolute and the relative as well as a primary/secondary distinction; and for so long as we make these distinctions *at all* we are still in a universe of discourse in which God comes first and theism occupies the high ground. I must confess that I myself have not yet found a satisfactory way of describing the new vision of the world and the new religious outlook that does not still secretly presuppose the primacy of the old God and the old world view. So I am stuck in an impossible intellectual love-relationship with an impossible God. And I'm not sure that I even *want* to be cured.

APPENDIX

Impossible love for the faith and the Church

We have seen that it is extraordinarily difficult to exorcize God completely from one's thinking—so difficult, indeed, that the most hard-bitten professional atheists often show themselves to be the most captivated by the God in whom they do not believe. The Oxford populariser of science Richard Dawkins, who so much riles the religious, turns out *himself* to cling determinedly to the traditional theistic foundations of Western thought: the Logos out there, objective Reality, objective Truth. Like most scientists, Dawkins is a closet theist.

Even those who have tried much harder to be consistent atheists have done very little better than Dawkins. Jacques Derrida, who made the most thoroughgoing and subtle attempt yet to expose and undermine those same theistic foundations, remained "haunted" by God, and will surely be remembered in the long run as a great religious thinker.

In a supposedly post-Christian world, many of those who have ostensibly rejected God not only still love God, but they also go on loving and clinging to much else that should have died for them when God died. Like Thomas Hardy, whose case we noted earlier, they find themselves suddenly discovering fresh interest and beauty in all the things that they ought to be giving up with God. They find that theological argument is interesting. They begin to love religious art—especially architecture and church music. They are filled with an immense and almost *Jewish* yearning sadness by the slow, long-drawn-out death of the Faith itself. Above all, they still love the idea of the Church as a supernatural society, the one society that you can really *believe in* and give your whole soul to, and the only society that includes the dead amongst its active members.

The Church is a *cosmic* society: an idea so compelling that people do not give it up lightly even though they freely admit that they are no longer anything like orthodox believers. The English writer Rose Macauley coined the term "Anglo-agnostic" to describe her own position—a position shared, I would say, by the minor poet John Betjeman—and several prominent "Anglo-atheists" inhabit today's Cambridge. They go to church and to their College Chapels, as the astronomer Sir Martin Rees puts it, "for historical and cultural reasons." Nobody expresses surprise.

In the early and mid-twentieth century a large number of British intellectuals—poets, composers, and visual artists—were well content to be generally perceived as believing Christians, even when their personal faith and practice fell a long way short of what that label would normally imply. This was true, for example, of poets like Eliot and Auden, of virtually all Catholic novelists, of composers from Britten to Tavener, and of painters like Stanley Spencer. Such figures were glad to be seen as belonging to the Christian tradition, even though they were much less orthodox than the general public supposed. Especially about God. Eliot may have been a churchwarden and a weekly communicant, but his worldview owed much more to F. H. Bradley's Idealist philosophy and to the Upanishads than to the Western Christian tradition. One need only check the treatment of God in the *Four Quartets*.

Today, the climate has changed. Christianity is very much out of fashion, and even admits *itself* that it is in rapid decline. The "impossible love" that clings to the Church and to its language and its music may be less common now, but it does still exist. Sometimes it is very intense. The novelist and biographer Andrew (A. N.) Wilson publicly broke with religion some fifteen years ago, but since then most of his very considerable literary output has been obsessively concerned with religion: it is a striking example of the way impossible love can be more stormy and passionate than the normal variety.

God begins to be really interesting and troublesome when he dies, and our religion begins to worry us more now that we have broken with it than it did when we felt able to take it for granted. That's impossible love for you.

Loves Lost or Out of the Question

T he human life-world is so large, so all-encompassing, and so varied that it easily accommodates people of wildly divergent views, all of whom severally and sincerely believe that their experience of life fully confirms their own opinions. To some, it seems that our lives are scripted in advance by God, predestined or fated down to the smallest detail. Nothing is merely accidental; everything has a purpose. But others take exactly the opposite view. They think that our lives are a string of accidents over which we have almost no control. We may as well take all our decisions by rolling a die.[20] It's been tried; and the novels, at least, suggest that it works about as well as trying to be "rational."

I suspect that, as everyday language suggests, most people take the intermediate view that with the help of self-discipline, regular habits, careful planning, and personal commitment to a vocation, a faith, or an ambition, one may frame and fulfil a personal life plan. It can be done, and sometimes it *is* done. But such people are in a rather small minority, and even they must always remain vulnerable to sickness, misfortune, and other hazards. Most people drift, waiting to see what will happen and hoping to be able to spot and seize something good if and when it presents itself. It is in some such spirit that many young women seem to wait for "The Right One" to come along, no doubt because social conventions seem to rule out any more active and assertive method of tracking him down and seizing him before somebody else snaps him up.

This raises the question of which sex is the more vulnerable to the caprice of fortune. If we think of the careers of our school and college contemporaries over the past twenty-five or fifty years, we will probably confess ourselves baffled. We could never have guessed in advance that this person would have such a big success and that one would fail so disastrously; that one should live such a safe, conventional life while another should change course so often and so dramatically. Nowadays one sees little difference between the sexes in these matters—except, perhaps, that men are a little more vulnerable to premature, accidental, or violent death, and women's success and happiness in life is more closely related to their good or ill fortune in love.

Interestingly, our religious tradition has always attempted to deny altogether the extent to which our fate in life is a matter of chance, and out of our control. The presumption has always been that God has the last word: God's good Providence controls everything, leaving nothing to chance. With the help of the Church's "means of Grace" we who are made in God's image must employ self-knowledge, self-mastery, and self-direction so that all our loves and aims are properly and rationally prioritized. Following the philosophical tradition, the religious life was above all a peaceful, orderly, *rational* life.

Very well, but we need examples. Who lives such a rational and examined life? The members of religious orders, surely, whose lives are designed to be as rational and stable as possible, and sheltered from the violent passions and chances of life in the world. No doubt many monks and nuns did live approximately the lives that orthodox theology seems to require of us, but of course even the cloister was sometimes invaded, and even the technically religious might prove vulnerable to temptation and fall into sin. The monks therefore prayed for deliverance both from external dangers and from internal temptations.

At the Reformation there began a serious attempt to hallow life "in the world," and especially domestic life. The compromise usually provided that in your private life you could and should live according to the high calling of the Gospel, whereas in your public, working life—whether as a public official or one plying a trade—you would do well if you lived by the precepts of the Old Testament Law. The domestic world was to be ruled by love, and the public world by the principles of justice.

The home thus became the direct successor to the monastery, and it was assumed that benign patriarchy was as normal and acceptable a form of government in the home as it was in the Church, in the State, and in the Cosmos at large. Because women spent most of their time at home, it was assumed until late-Victorian times that they were the more consistently Christian of the two sexes. The modest, sober dress of wives and widows, and the regular routines of domestic life—including daily prayers and Grace at meals—perpetuated the older style of religious life within the home.

This system of thought extolled above all else order, stability, and peace—under the aegis of God—in all the various spheres of life. Writers concerned with the religious life and morality paid little or no attention to the brief, harsh, and often violent nature of the lives of most of the laboring masses. Except as objects of charity, these unfortunates did not merit anyone's close attention. Orthodox writers were generally so busy praising reason and order that their accounts of the religious life tell us nothing about how we are to cope with all the violent irruptions of irrationality, frustration, disappointment, misfortune, and woe that trouble actual people. The believer simply prayed to God to be delivered from troubles of all kinds:

> O God, who knowest us to be set in the midst of so many and great dangers, that by reason of the frailty of our nature we cannot always stand upright: Grant to us such strength and protection, as may support us in all dangers, and carry us through all temptations.[21]

God was reason and order, and we were thought to have been so constituted as to be happiest when our "unruly wills and affections" are brought back into their proper god-ordained order. It was recognized that even the regenerate may still be troubled by flickers of concupiscence or other inordinate desires, and therefore they must pray for the strength to resist temptation, and for Grace to straighten them out.

In our time it is so widely assumed that all religious belief is irrational that we are taxed to remember how very rationalist was orthodox religion's account of human nature and the good life. Since religion was about social control, God was reason and order; and the world-process was governed in every detail by an all-powerful, just, wise, and benevolent Providence. Trouble of every kind, whether endogenously arising in the form of temptation, or exogenously threatening us in the form of external dangers, was a form of disorder that needed to be got back under the benign, patriarchal government of reason. As for happiness and life-satisfaction, the presumption was that you would have it if only you lived in accordance with God's will, and managed to get your own psychological makeup into the sort of order that God intended for it.

We modern people seem to inhabit a very different world, and in this present discussion we are bringing together a large group of seemingly irrational regrets, disappointments, conflicts, personal upheavals, and hopeless yearnings that play a large part in our lives, but were simply not recognized or provided for within "the religious life" as it was traditionally conceived. That omission we now need to rectify. As for our forebears, if they ever felt as troubled as we are by a sense of life's myriad missed opportunities, contradictions, unconsoled griefs, and longings, they merely assumed that God would put it all right for them beyond the grave. They believed in a universal Restoration of all things (*apocatastasis*) at the end of time: the dead would be raised, all wrongs would be righted, and all losses made good. The nearest equivalent to that hope that we can find in our present culture is the view, held by some proponents of the "possible-worlds" theory, that all possible worlds are actual.[22] Thus, if I am not happy about the way some particular event has gone for me, I can console myself with the thought that in various other worlds things will have turned out better.

It's not a very consoling idea. It doesn't really say any more than that things might have gone otherwise. As for us here and now, our losses, missed opportunities, and disappointments are eternal. We can expect no Apocatastasis, no Restoration at the end of time.[23] Everything that passes away (and everything *does* pass away) is gone forever.

Hence the heightened sadness of our lost loves, unborn children, and missed opportunities. If we nowadays cannot help but see our own lives as long chains of contingencies that are only rather imperfectly unified, neither can we escape the awareness of a continuous slipping-away of unfulfilled possibilities. This is a theme well-suited to the cinema, and often met there: note, for example, films like *It's a Wonderful Life* (Frank Capra, 1945), *Sliding Doors* (Peter Hewitt, 1997), and *The Family Man* (Brett Ratner, 2000), which describe how minor contingencies and spur-of-the-moment decisions open up and then block off other paths our lives could have taken. Many of them have to do with sexual love, a topic that bulks large nowadays but which our religious tradition was never able to treat seriously. The religious tradition—at any rate, after the later Middle Ages and the Reformation—did eventually become able to acknowledge the propriety of rational affection within the family, but love, serious *love*, was too capricious and overwhelming to fit into its world-view.

Consider an example. A male student friend and contemporary of mine fell deeply in love at the age of about twenty five. Unfortunately he was shy, and before he got around to making any serious move the young woman in question had become somebody else's girlfriend—and was lost to him eternally. His friends—of whom I was one—saw what was happening, but we were too young and dim-witted to understand how much was at stake. Thereafter, he did not marry for over forty years. Instead he followed the orthodox route by living a celibate life of devoted service, for which he eventually won some public recognition. But his whole life was blighted beyond recompense. I was there, and I did nothing.

Corresponding stories about women who pined away like patience on a monument[24] because their men never came are a literary cliché: Mariana in her moated grange, *Madama Butterfly*, Christina Rossetti, *The French Lieutenant's Woman* . . . one could go on indefinitely. Here the theme is complicated by the extraordinary persistence of the social or psychological convention that decrees it fatal for the woman to make the first move. Her sexual power can be exerted only by passivity and indirection. She must wait, impeccably groomed, patient, and very crafty. The same idea is taken much futher in the recent writings of Doris Lessing (born 1919), starting with *Love, Again* (1996), in which Lessing applies her formidable talent and courage to the almost-taboo topic of an older woman who falls head over heels in love with two young men, one after another.

Here the conventions that condemn the woman to silence and passivity are at their most rigid. She must never "let herself go," as people put it. She must at all times be very, very controlled—cool, composed and smiling. But, poor thing, she is long past the menopause, and she herself wonders what on earth can be the biological function of the capacity to fall so much in love at such an advanced age. As for other people, she knows that even the most cautious and heavily-veiled expression of her true feelings will be met only by acute embarrassment and pity. She is condemned to utter silence: her love is about as impossible as any love can be. What can she *do* with it? Can she put her passion to any possible use, or does she just have to repress it and suffer?

In this particular case, the world seems to be much harder on women than on men. After all, when people see a young trophy wife on the arm of a wealthy and powerful man in his early seventies, they merely smile indulgently, and speculate about whether even he can be vain enough to expect her to be faithful for more than a token period. But an important general issue is involved here, too: love means an enormous amount to us, and plays a big part in our lives. It is notoriously wayward, easily fixing upon highly inappropriate objects, and easily deflected into highly imprudent channels. It is unpredictable, and very difficult for even the most sober and inherently monogamous people to manage. And the upshot of all this is that in real life we find that *most of our loves are of the "impossible" kind*—a state of affairs that is as odd as it is awkward. Modern Western society is post-Freudian and very knowing. There is little remaining segregation of the sexes, and it is customary to find men and women mingling freely and informally in almost all areas of life. Predictably, Eros is very active; but at the same time nearly everyone is also conscious of the great long-term value of stable monogamous relationships— nearly always heterosexual. Inevitably, then, since marriage—the one really "possible" kind of love—tends to be exclusive, most others are of necessity "impossible." How often we find ourselves remembering lost loves from the past that have been made "impossible" by the mere passage of time; how often we are lured by current "impossible" loves that are tugging at us.

The problem has become more acute in recent decades. Until about fifty years ago there was still a good deal of sexual segregation. Most men, frankly, preferred the company of other men and regarded women as being less important; most women, too, preferred the company of other women. There was chronic mild mistrust between the sexes—something that many great writers from Shakespeare to Nietzsche tried to make the best of by declaring that a little mutual antagonism between the sexes was an aphrodisiac. It added a touch of spice or even intriguing darkness to their relationship. So it was claimed, but in retrospect a great many men of that period seem to have been heterosexual misogynists. They married women, but never really *liked* them. They were apt to follow the precepts of their classical education and regard Eros as a malady. Such men often saw a visit to a brothel as a cheaper and less troublesome way of satisfying their sexual needs than the whole complicated farrago of love and marriage. As one Victorian literary man, Samuel Butler, put it, "Why buy the whole cow, when all you need is a pint of milk?"

Such men, of whom there used to be a great many, were simply unacquainted with deep heterosexual love of the kind that is a major spiritual force in our life. They did not like or respect women enough for serious love ever to become an issue for them. In today's much less segregated world, it is only too easy to get to like the opposite sex all too much. It is as if Eros is always stirring, and as if we live in a state in which Eros is always about to rise up and fix upon an object. At any one time there is always someone with whom I am in danger of falling in love. It is as if all our social life is now rather *flirtatious,* and is lived permanently on the brink of getting to be rather more serious than that. It is as if we are all respectable married folk who nevertheless enjoy going out to be eyed and chatted up.

How, then, do we keep a moral balance? The modern emancipation of women and the resulting ease with which the sexes mingle collaborate to enable close heterosexual friendships; and historically speaking this is a great moral achievement. If in addition we attach high value to heterosexual attraction and even higher value to deep heterosexual love, then how are we to maintain faithful long-term monogamous relationships? It is surely "impossible" to regard every extra-marital flicker of Eros as a temptation to be sternly resisted on the grounds that it may lead to an "impossible" love.

At this point we find ourselves caught in a conflict between *two* impossibles! Since Eros cannot be simply affirmed or denied, we face a grave yet very common dilemma. But at least it is less tragic than the classic case of a deep and serious love that is quite out of the question, namely incestuous love. Such utterly impossible love really does happen, and it has been the subject of great drama; but mercifully it is rare.

APPENDIX
Impossible love for an animal

S—is a young woman who has always liked animals, and who discovered when young the strange delight that can come from being carried away by playing with an animal. A week before writing this, I was with her at Linton Zoo, south of Cambridge, where there is at present a single Grevy's Zebra in a one-acre paddock. This surprisingly large and formidable animal, with its extended, stiff and crest-like mane, came up to its fence and followed S—along as she walked by. Seeing the end of the fence approaching, S—turned about sharply and walked back. The animal did the same, and then suddenly a high-spirited dance developed, in which the zebra showed extraordinary enthusiasm in copying every movement S—made. After a few minutes they both stopped to rest, standing close together on opposite sides of the wire.

Next day S—was worried: should she go back to see the zebra again? Had this intense few minutes of exhilarated communion created some kind of continuing *obligation*? Of course not. That sort of love for an animal is almost as rare as the highly endangered Grevy's Zebra itself, and nothing can ever "come" of it. It's impossible.

I should add, very briefly, that love for a domesticated animal is of course common and easy—but only because the domesticated animal has been specially trained by us to live with us as a companion. Zebras, by contrast, are notoriously impossible to domesticate and ill-tempered. Hence my uneasiness, and astonishment, at S-'s "impossible" communion with the Grevy's Zebra. Yet such moments, when we look in wonder across an impassable barrier, do sometimes happen to us.

The Impossible Ideal

R eaders may be wondering why I have not previously referred to two celebrated treatments of the theme of a middle-aged intellectual led to disaster by his own infatuation with an infinitely desirable but elusive, and indeed forbidden, love-object. They are of course Thomas Mann's *Der Tod in Venedig* (1913), translated as *Death in Venice* (1928), and Vladimir Nabokov's *Lolita* (1955, 1959). The Thomas Mann novella was memorably filmed by Luchino Visconti (1971), but censorship problems seem to have dogged all attempts to film *Lolita*, the best of which was Stanley Kubrick's 1961 production.

Troublesome though the question of censorship has been, I suggest that neither work is primarily about sexual love. The Thomas Mann story is about the decline of European civilization, and the fatality of a vocation to art in a world in which art ceases to have any real place. In every way Gustav Aschenbach is, as they say, **losing it**. Think what an extraordinary number of the most talented American poets, novelists, and painters came to a bad end during the twentieth century. And as for *Lolita*, was it not written in the heyday of America's world-conquering youth and innocence? Lolita is America itself, consumerist America—so easy, so seductive, so effortlessly sure of itself and so infinitely superior to her tired old European partner. Even today it is impossible to visit America and go touring in a rented car without succumbing to its charm. Just try making it a *white* car, and drive over the Golden Gate in bright sunshine with the radio pumping out American pop music—and you will be lost. It is a cliché, it is obvious, and it is quite irresistible. *Lolita* is about the new world of American consumerism, and its effect upon the old world of European civilization. The very expert erotic writing pairs typical representatives of the two, and of course a fatality occurs: Hubert Humbert must come to a bad end. Until quite recently Europe was still capable of very great achievement, but its long decline continues, and has no doubt been accelerated by its infatuation with the new world that has succeeded it.

Death in Venice and *Lolita*, then, are about fatal attractions, impossible ideals blindly pursued. For a theological analogue of such a self-destructive obsession, one might propose the often compulsive quest for *purity* that in the past has played a crucial role in religious and moral thinking—and not least in Platonism and monasticism.

In traditional prescientific thinking it was common to see the cosmic order as having been established by first drawing lines of distinction between different zones or regions and then stocking each region with a full set of appropriate natural kinds, each of which breeds "true to type."[25] To cite a simple biblical example, "beasts of the field" go on four legs, "birds of the air" have feathered wings, and "fishes of the sea" come equipped with scales and fins. Creatures that do not quite fit this scheme—snakes, bats, and eels, for example—are likely to be seen as anomalous and therefore "unclean." In general one should respect the cosmic order, and any crossing of a major boundary is apt to be risky. Among the most important of such boundaries is the surface of one's own body. Anything that enters or leaves the body—as happens with eating, excretion, menstruation, sex, childbirth, being wounded, and so on—is a potential source of ritual uncleanness. It was strongly believed that in order to remain healthy both humans and animals needed to remain "purebred." Hybrids are unclean—and therefore often infertile.

This ancient scheme of thought still affects our language and even our behavior. It helped to create the traditional belief that one could become holier and more pleasing to God by practicing celibacy or by fasting. More recently, it has influenced nationalism and similar political movements by leading people to attach great merit to racial segregation and ethnic purity, or to mount campaigns for moral purity. The tidiness that wants "everything in its place" and nothing *out of* place (literally, *obscene*) is similarly motivated. So is an excessive devotion to hygiene and disinfectants.

Historically, then, the religious person was supposed to be fastidious, to wear white, to be very clean, to draw back a little from the exchanges of life, and to avoid any "promiscuous" mingling that risked contamination. Holiness, separation, and purity were effectively equated and pursued obsessively, in the belief that the purest and most isolated is the healthiest and holiest. Hence the convents of nuns.

No doubt there were always some who thought that if you pursued ritual cleanliness and purity too single-mindedly you might actually *weaken* the stock by becoming "inbred," or you might become so scrupulous and timorous as to be almost incapable of action. But the underlying assumption—that it's better not to mix different natures, that separation and purity are better than mingling—has proved amazingly persistent. It is still with us, as one sees in the public outcry against genetically modified crops that might either "contaminate" other foods being grown nearby, or prove to be "bad" for us. But in the light of modern biology the quest for uncontaminated purity and the belief in clear and distinct essences are utter nonsense. Life is a flowing process of chemical, sexual, genetic and symbolic exchanges, and health is normally associated with mingling rather than strict segregation. It is a mistake and a waste of time to look for a pure timeless essence of Christianity, or the quiddity of Welshness.

Closely associated with the pursuit of uncontaminated purity is the belief in various sorts of "identity." These include *first*, the belief in my own distinct and permanent personal identity—my soul, my core-self, the real me; *second*, the belief in a predestined vocation in life already prepared for me—my calling, my fate, my task, my destiny; and *third*, the belief in a predestined partner—someone ready-made for me and awaiting me somewhere out there, my soulmate, my one and only, my better half, the love of my life.

These beliefs about personal identity—a true self, a predestined partner, a mission in life—can also take a collective form, as when people create and seek to realize myths of national identity, national destiny, and national entitlement to sovereignty over a particular territory.

As we have already shifted the focus once, from "purity" to "identity," so we may now shift it again: from purity to dreams of unrestricted freedom and independence. Here it becomes even more obvious that what people are demanding—whether on their own behalf as individuals or for their "nation"—is something quite impossible. The rhetoric is always unqualified, and therefore calls for total emancipation, even to the point of self-sufficiency and isolation. Suppose a skeptic asks a radical nationalist, "Are you really demanding complete independence? May no persons or communications or electronic money or goods ever cross your frontiers?" The latter will splutter that of course he doesn't quite mean that—but still he will not say exactly what he *does* mean. And that shows that he does not intend to admit publicly the mythical, "impossible" character of all dreams of total personal and national "liberation."

Here we have moved onto territory first explored by sceptical, right-wing thinkers. Nietzsche was one of the first to point out the extent to which, in the late-modern democratic epoch, political life and action are still driven by myths. Later right-wing skeptics such as Leo Strauss and the British maverick politician Enoch Powell have hastened to add that the wise man does not therefore recoil fastidiously from politics. On the contrary, he will understand and exploit the illusions that people live by (my own people, my tribe, my nation, my race, my class, my religious group, oppressed but now struggling for its liberation, and so on and on), and he will do this in order to create outlets for people's energies, new structures of authority, and above all some quiet spaces where philosophers can continue to live and do their work undisturbed.

It is not only at the political level that people continue to live by such cherished and necessary myths as that of the "nation": they do the same at the individual level. For example, most people still attach great importance to genealogy and to their own lineal descendants—even though marriage is a much weakened institution, the transmission of surnames has become notably irregular, and we all recognize that the traditional "family tree" reflects an outmoded patriarchal ideology. Recently I found myself extraordinarily pleased to have at last a delightful grandson who bears my surname. This infant is the latest in "the line," the firstborn son of a firstborn son, and so on for at least five generations back; and the other surviving members of my family who bear the name Cupitt are as pleased as I am to see "the name" continue for another generation. Perhaps they are thinking of how pleased my father would have been if he were still alive. I know I am. Rationally, I know that "the Cupitts" as a direct male lineage are not *really* a group of more-or-less identical chaps. After five generations, it doesn't really mean very much. After all, my grandson has only one-sixteeth of his genes (including of course that stumpy Y-chromosome) in common with my grandfather. Lineage is more than a bit mythical, really. Nevertheless, these ideas that meant so much to our ancestors for millennia still mean surprisingly much to me, in spite of my awareness that they are mythical. But then, all of us remain obstinately attached to a number of prescientific cultural fictions, and still draw comfort from them even though we know that they are mythical. We do not *really* "live on" in our descendants—or at least, we certainly don't do so for long.

What of other impossible ideals? Recent changes in philosophy and the general growth of knowledge have deprived us of most of them. I don't believe in the saint, the perfect human being. There is no such animal, not after Freud. To be sure, we know of outstanding human beings with extraordinary gifts, but they are in no way different *in kind* from the rest of us. On the contrary, a modern biography will always show that their gifts and achievements were rooted in exactly the same biological makeup as ours. Similarly, just as nowadays people no longer look back nostalgically to an age of original innocence in a perfect world or forward to a future state of universal human liberation in a finally perfected world, so we as individuals never imagine we ever were perfect in the past or will become so in the future. Similarly, just as liberal democracy is demythologized politics that has become a matter of improvisation and perpetual tinkering, so ethics has *also* been demythologized. One strives for a more kindly and humane world, one does one's best in little things, one improvises in response to social change—but the grand dreams of final salvation and perfection are all dead, and therefore do not need further discussion here. They, at least, represent impossible ideals that we have successfully given up.

This prompts an observation with which to conclude the present review of our impossible loves. During the past fifty years the dominant cultural forces (apart from our unprecedented prosperity and our consumerism) have been evolutionary biology and the increasing dominance of high technology, even in everyday life. These cultural forces have gravely weakened both our sense of history and our cultural idealism. We find ourselves stripped bare, and forced back upon the basic facts of the human life-cycle: man and woman, sex and childbirth, love and death, growing up and growing old, and the cycle of the generations.

Elsewhere I have used the phrase "the return of the great questions" for the way that the end of metaphysics and dogmatic religious belief has taken us back to the beginnings of the Western tradition, and to the way in which the first philosophers at that time confronted the bare facts of the human condition. In our present discussion we have met the practical and ethical counterpart of the same shift: high cultural idealism is dead; and once again man and woman, sex and babies, love and death are **what it's all about**.

Life As a Chapter
of Accidents

Before long, someone must attempt the first history of life, reviewing the manifold ways in which people have seen life and their own lives in different periods and under the influence of different systems of thought.

The most obvious contrast, one vividly reflected in many idioms in ordinary language, is that between those who see their lives largely or in every detail destined—whether by God or the Fates or by physical necessity—and those who believe human affairs to be governed by blind chance—a doctrine that comes in both comic and tragic versions.

People often forget it, but mainstream philosophical and theological monotheism was always predestinarian. God was the sole creator and first cause of everything. All-powerful, all-wise, and all-good, he had total control over the whole world-process. Everything is foreseen and foreordained by him, and everything is orchestrated towards the fulfilment of God's good purpose for his whole Creation. Your own life is readable as the story of your pre-destined progress towards either final salvation or final damnation within the larger overall design. God has created you a free agent, of course, but he has also foreseen the use you will make of your freedom, so that by your free action you never frustrate God's will: you merely implement it. You act freely when you act in a rational way that is an authentic expression of your own nature, and when you are not under external duress. Thus you are still justly judged and condemned for your own sins because they were true expressions of your own nature, even though (since God had made you that way) you could not have done otherwise.

The crucial point here is that in this vision of the world, nothing is "meaningless" or merely accidental. When you look back over your own life, if you have faith and are one of the Elect, you will be able to see the whole story as revealing the guiding hand of Divine Providence. But if the whole of your life as it has actually happened was pre-ordained by Divine Providence, it couldn't have happened otherwise than it did, and there is no reason whatever to waste any time in worrying about lost loves, broken ideals and missed opportunities. The only thing that has any reality and any religious significance is the way things have actually happened. Speculation about what might have been is therefore quite useless, and even sinful. You will simply not give it any attention: it is of no real interest at all. It is at this point that we understand how and why Calvinism—the version of Christian theology that has made the most of these themes—is so positivistic, so philistine, and so uninterested in speculation. Whatever has been and whatever is now and must be simply is the Will of God. So act upon *it* alone: all else is vain, and quite unreal.

We see now why strong dogmatic religious belief shields people of faith from the great questions of life. They already *know* all the answers in a way that leaves no room for regrets, or complaints, or dreams. They will not be at all interested in our impossible loves, and they cordially disapprove of fantasy, fiction, and most art. They do not believe in chance, and if they are consistent they will not seek any insurance "cover." They will simply believe in Providence, and leave it at that.

Those who are not drawn to the theological version of determinism may be influenced by the old pagan Fatalism, according to which unseen supernatural powers control our destiny. Or they may be attracted by some form of mechanistic determinism based on the belief that Newtonian physics—or something very like it—can in principle give a complete account of all events in the physical world. But the practical consequences of these two views are very much the same as those of theological determinism: if the way things happen to go is always, from a larger and better-informed point of view the way they *must* go, and if there was never any real question of anything turning out otherwise than it has done and is doing, then we should not waste time on regrets, or dreams, or lost loves. There was never any real prospect of your life taking any other course than it has. Whether under God or fatalism or mechanistic determinism, the actual is always the necessary, and it is all we need ever think about.

The major alternative vision of life has in modern times been very greatly influenced by Darwinism, and perhaps especially since the 1930s by "neo-darwinism", with an additional boost from molecular biology since the structure of DNA was unravelled in the early 1950s. Life on the largest scale, the entire evolutionary process, has begun to look like a chapter of accidents—accidents which include not only genetic mutations, but also major geological events such as Ice Ages, cataclysmic earthquakes, and climate-altering volcanic eruptions—along with several disastrous meteorite impacts. In addition, it is now well-understood that Darwin's famous metaphor of "natural selection" describes a process, namely the struggle to survive and to reproduce, that operates as a means of selection *without there being any selector*. Darwin's brilliant, terrifying idea is quite *radically* opposed to all notions of a hidden hand of Providence first designing and then guiding the course of world-events. Darwin himself intended to demolish forever the "intelligent design" way of looking at the adaptation of organisms to their environment.[26] To their credit, Evangelical Protestants are honest and correct in their recognition that if Darwin is right, they are dead in the water. Liberal Protestants and Roman Catholics have done much less well: they have made a very coarse and unfortunate strategic error in attempting to claim that Darwinian evolution is compatible with ethical theism. It simply is not. Unwisely, they were trying to postpone the inevitable reckoning that has now come upon them. Only the young Nietzsche had the intelligence to react appropriately to Darwin's ideas as soon as he understood them. His reaction could be summarized thus: "I don't like Darwin's ideas at all. But he is obviously broadly correct. Therefore God is dead. We need a new kind of human being, who can bear the truth. And we need a new religious thought." It is as simple as that; so simple that only a major genius could see it. So simple that my esteemed colleagues in the theological world cannot see it yet. Or even if they *can* see it, they are certainly not going to say it out loud.

Fortunately, ordinary people and ordinary language have by now largely understood what has happened to us. We have come to recognize that our life really *is* radically contingent. We are, and our life is, contingent all the way down and in every respect. We just happen to be here, and that for only a short while, and when we have gone (which may not be very long now) the fact that we were here will not have made any lasting difference at all.

A philosophical novel commonly invoked in this regard is Sartre's *La Nauseé*, 1938 (*Nausea* 1949), with often-quoted passages describing the central character's sense of the utter, and almost obscene, gratuitousness of finite existence. Much better, though, is Joseph Heller's *Something Happened* (1974), in which the philosophical crisis is not objectified but is described as it grows *within the subjectivity* of the central character, Bob Slocum. He is a prosperous, comfortable American suburban man. He has everything: life for him is as easy as it has ever been for anyone. But throughout the novel he gradually becomes more and more troubled by abyssal feelings of fear, spiritual desolation, meaninglessness, absurdity, and dread—until at the end of the book something happens, something merely accidental but utterly tragic and grotesquely horrible.

What Heller describes is a variant of the theme that we have already described as "the return of the great questions." As the old religious cosmology passes away, taking with it the entire apparatus of organized religion, human beings are slowly deprived of all the beautiful and comforting old illusions that used to shield them from too naked a view of the truth about our human situation. "The Great Questions of Life," long set aside, now return with a vengeance. In the European tradition they become increasingly prominent and troubling from Shakespeare and Pascal onwards, and especially in nineteenth-century pessimism after Schopenhauer. One thinks of Thomas Hardy and Paul Gauguin: What are we? What's it all about?

Joseph Heller's novel invites us to see all these issues raised in an even more terrifying form by the way things have gone during the half-century or so since World War Two. It has been an epoch of enormous prosperity and of consumerism. Consumerism specializes above all in pleasing the customer, especially in identifying people's needs, wants, desires, and dissatisfactions—and then meeting them in full. In a consumer society the entire social system is geared to making life as easy for us in every respect as human ingenuity can make it. In North America, in Australia, and in one or two other places, this has been done. There, life for most has become amazingly easy: indeed, it has *remained* so, for the suburban way of life lived by two-thirds of the whole U. S. population has changed only very slowly during the past fifty or sixty years.

Here is ordinary human life made comfortable, secure, and innocently confident of its own goodness. The system has recognized and met all the needs that it *can* recognize and meet. Surely life is now, as the phrase goes, "No problem!" Unfortunately, it is just at this point where all the identifiable needs have been recognized and met, that we at last become fully demythologized, see life for what it is—its metaphysical Emptiness, its temporality, its contingency, its finitude—and get the horrors. Heller, like the young Kierkegaard, thinks the chief horror is fear of finite existence in and of itself.

That is why so many, Americans in particular, still cling so desperately to a religion that no longer works and cannot help them. They correctly recognize that the problem of life is a religious problem, and therefore they understandably conclude that the best thing for them to do in the face of our post-modern spiritual crisis of meaninglessness and emptiness is to go back to their spiritual roots in reformed Protestantism.

Alas, the ecclesiastical Christianity that we have inherited cannot help. It doesn't cut deep enough. It's about sin and redemption, it's about the Church (i. e., about spiritual power and social control), and it's about the work of projecting a slide-show of pictures and stories in order to conceal the Void and protect ordinary people from seeing the bleak truth about the human situation. But today even ordinary people *have already seen* the Void, and the old painted curtain cannot be drawn back again to recreate the old illusions. No, after people have become comprehensively *dis*illusioned they cannot go back again to their previous state of innocence. That is why Church Christianity, despite its best efforts, is unable to understand and address the peculiar spiritual crisis we now face: nihilism, extreme boredom and extreme terror mixed, utter spiritual desolation and meaninglessness, coupled with the knowledge that I am hurtling toward a final extinction which may engulf me at any moment, and certainly will engulf me before very long.

The crisis arises from our painful and vivid awareness of the utter contingency of everything, together with its temporality and finitude. Everything is sheerly contingent, gratuitous, a might-not-have-been. No threads of necessary connexion, or of "real" and objective purpose, or meaning, or value glue the world together—unless we have created them for ourselves. Only we, only the stories that *we* tell in our science, our history and our religion, only *we* supply the glue that sticks the world together and gives to it such narrative and intellectual continuity as it seems to us to have. The odd and sad truth is that the demythologizing process that has been slowly but inexorably going on since the Enlightenment has left us demoralized. Every culture projects a world, and we used to believe fervently in the world that *we* projected. A few of us (principally, the scientists) still believe in it. But when we lose our old innocent realistic faith, we seem to become dispirited and to lack the creative will and energy to create and project a new and better world. We are left gloomily contrasting the old world—solid, single, and laid on for us by God—with our self-made new world that we fear can never be more than a fragile, fleeting consensus, one of a number of possibilities that by chance happens to have been realized.

So much for the late-modern view of our life as a chapter of accidents, and in particular for the pessimistic interpretation of it. What of the possibility of a comic and optimistic interpretation of life's tumbling, excessive chanciness and brevity?

Such an interpretation has always been possible. It is rooted in the world of the broadest comedy, of "low life" and the very poor, who are everywhere the most ardent devotees of the goddess Fortuna. The poorest live, as it has been said, "in the kingdom of necessity," and they naturally like to keep alive the possibility that chance may deliver them via a lottery ticket. In the picaresque novel, the hero is a likeable rogue, a survivor who lives through many sudden and violent reversals of fortune. Ordinary people are pleased by that: they like the idea that things might very easily have turned out, and might yet turn out, very differently from the way they look at the moment.

There is more to be said. Ordinary people are just as acutely aware as intellectuals of the terror and the horror of contingent, finite existence; but whereas intellectuals (especially since Schopenhauer) have always tended to develop gloomy and pessimistic philosophies, ordinary people's preference is almost always for laughter, even about the least funny topics. Hence the great philosophical interest of gallows and graveyard humour, black humour, sick humour, politically-incorrect humour, "grossout" humour, humour of bad taste, dark humour, obscene and scatological humour, surreal and perverse nonsense, and all the rest. Such material often arouses great indignation and disapproval from people of "Establishment" views, who live in a much more secure and stable world with relatively secure and stable values. But we who on the whole live in that relatively secure world should understand that "the less fortunate" have had to develop their own ways of coping with the dark side of life. They have found that broad laughter works best; the broader and more derisive, the better.

Perhaps in modern times the terms of the argument have been shifting, anyway. Orthodox theism and Newtonian physics tended to be realistic and deterministic: things can turn out only one way—namely, *this* way, the way they *have* turned out. But since Kant and Hegel, and since Darwin and the rise of modern physics, the old cut-and-dried, hard-edged vision of the world—and of the way our language could delineate the world—has broken down. Notions of randomness and chance play a much more prominent part in our central scientific theories now, and in philosophy it no longer looks as if we have a ready-made, fully determinate objective world that is prior to our language and can be accurately manifested in it. No, the situation is rather that the objective world is no more than a jumble of jostling possibilities until our language and our theory come along and (as the phrase goes) **make something of it**. What is more, there is always much room for differences of interpretation, so that in the general conversation of humanity two themes are always playing against each other. On the one hand, we have a great need to establish and maintain a common vision of the world so that we can "do business" with each other, while on the other hand each of us is all the time trying—as artists do—to promote his or her own personal vision of the world.[27]

There is always this conflict between order and freedom, between the claims of society and the claims of individual creativity. As a result, we now have a culture in which reality itself is much less cut-and-dried than it used to be, and in which different interpretations of the world and visions of life are constantly at play. Inevitably, then, we are highly aware of divergent angles and perspectives, and of different ways things might have gone and might yet go. There is no longer such a sharp contrast between the actual and the merely possible as there used to be in the older, more "realistic" and deterministic visions of the world.

And *that*, I think, is why our "impossible loves" have become so prominent in our lives. Under the older and more predestinarian vision, they were a waste of time. You scarcely gave them a thought. But today they are very prominent. They are part of "the truth"—such as it is—about us and our world. The religious life used to be a matter of eschewing fanciful speculation, getting your head down, donning a uniform, and following a regular, almost military discipline. That was an appropriate form of religious life for a Universe of which there was in the end only one correct description, only one great capital-T Truth. Today, the religious life is increasingly more plural, ruminative, speculative. I find that I need to go on thinking about (and even communing with) a whole range of forever-lost people, gods, loves, hopes, and ideals. They are part of me, and always will be. They are selves I might have become, loves I might have pursued successfully, gods I might still be worshipping, dead people who (in some cases) might still be with me.

Mention of "the selves I might have been" reminds us that although they are objects that with the passage of time have become "impossible," they are not fittingly described as "love-objects." Nevertheless, they do deserve consideration here. If I believed myself to have been predestined by God to be exactly where and what I am today, then I would not waste any time in thinking about other selves I might have become. But it *does* seem to me that at various points in my past life I made snap decisions that drastically affected the whole course of my life thenceforward.

There was a day in the early 1970s when I answered the telephone—and suddenly found myself at a parting of the ways. Did I want eventually to become a church leader, with all the constraints and the compensations of that path; or did I want to remain an academic and devote myself more than anything else to a lifelong attempt to develop and clarify my own thinking—with all the concomitant perils of that very different path? I made a snap decision, and have always professed to have no regrets. But I certainly *could* have jumped the other way, and nowadays I cannot help wondering how it would have been with me if I had become that very different person in a very different world. Only a few years later that other path had become quite impossible, rather in the way that with marriage partners and other loves a missed opportunity may soon become an "eternal" impossibility; but the fact that these other selves, loves, and lives were for a time real possibilities for us keeps them alive in our memories. Contingently, I happen to have let all the other possibilities escape and become impossible; and also contingently, I happen to have become this self who writes these words. But the fact is—and let's try to grasp this point clearly—that whereas in a predestinate Universe there is only *one* truth about me, *one* life I live, and *one* self that I have become, in today's utterly contingent universe, with its complicated interplay of many customs and chances and choices, I, Don Cupitt today, am a thin coloured line of actual life-events rather fuzzily accompanied and surrounded by a whole bundle of other possible lives I might have lived and selves I might have become.

It is true that despite all my troubles I have often said that I refuse to express regret or to make any complaint, and certainly I believe that we must learn to say Amen to our actual lives and actual selves as they have turned out. But all those unfulfilled possibilities do seem to haunt us, like our lost children. They really do—and this perhaps explains why it is that since about the time of the French Revolution fictions of many kinds have come so to dominate the arts and popular culture. We need those stories, because they help us to understand and to develop various aspects of ourselves that we have lost or forfeited or neglected.

8

The Impossible and the Supernatural

I n *Impossible God: Derrida's Theology*, Hugh Rayment-Pickard attributes to Derrida a theology of God's impossibility. It sounds at first a highly paradoxical idea, but then we are reminded of a point on which Derrida and ordinary language essentially agree: when you try to rule something out as being impossible, the very vocabulary in which you rule it out has a way of ensuring that it returns and continues to haunt you—as if excluding it from the everyday world has the unexpected side-effect of endowing it with a sort of ghostly existence. Thereafter, you **can't get it out of your mind**: its very absence seems to keep turning into a constant, reproachful, shadowy presence.[28] Could it be that the impossible in our modern experience is turning into a new version of the old supernatural realm?

Morality offers a very obvious and familiar analogy: when we forbid something categorically, our very prohibition makes it into something interesting and tempting, something that fascinates people.[29] "Did he really *mean* to forbid it? Perhaps he's only forbidding it in order to provoke us into finding a way of doing it? After all, unless a thing *can* be done and is something that many people would certainly *want* to do, there wouldn't have been any point in forbidding it, would there?" So as every parent knows, forbidding X soon becomes a way of ensuring that X gets done, because to forbid something is unavoidably to draw attention to it as something that *can* be done. As they used to say of the Irish, "The only way to get them to speak their own language would be to ban it." So it might be that when we avow atheism and declare God to be impossible, by our act we provoke other people and ourselves into looking for rhetorical devices by which we can *get round* the denial, and find a way of ascribing to God an invisible, supernatural sort of existence. After all, in ordinary language the impossible is more or less the same thing as the forbidden: to declare something impossible is to say emphatically: "You can't do that!" But if I can say clearly just what it is that can't be done, it must at least be *logically* possible to do it. And don't we all nowadays get the impression that atheists think and talk about God more often than believers do—as if by their denial they have condemned themselves to being perpetually haunted by the God in whom they do not believe? Almost always the atheist has a much clearer idea of what it is that he *doesn't* believe than the believer has of what it is that he *does* believe. Perhaps you would care to explain now the sense in which God is *more real* to the atheist than he is to the believer?[30]

I think you see an answer: it is the same sense as that in which my own beloved parents are more real to me now than they were when they were alive. They have both died, and there is no life after death. But, precisely by being dead, they have become "eternally" and unchangingly enthroned in my consciousness so that I think of them daily now—which I didn't when I was busy and they were alive sixty miles away. They are with me all the time, silent benign presences looking down on me, and they do not age any further. They are forever exactly the same as they were just before they died. They are in eternity. So in our love for them, the dead are enthroned eternally, *more influential in their non-existence* than they were when alive.

That then is the sense in which nowadays the whole realm of the impossible has much in common with the supernatural world of traditional religion; and it explains how a dead God, impossible and therefore non-existent, can nevertheless continue to function as our god, eternally enthroned in our hearts—exactly, we may imagine, as the dead Egyptian Pharaoh, united with Osiris in the Underworld or in his sarcophagus, continued to be the king and to sustain the State. Well, the world of the dead always *was* the same world as the world of the gods, was it not? The dead no longer exist and God does not exist, but they both remain unchangingly present to us and part of our vocabulary. We still love them: they are perhaps the chief among our impossible loves, and as such they remain "sort-of-real."

Derrida's theology of an impossible God who doesn't exist but will always haunt us is an excellent example of the "minimalist" philosophies of religion that are being put forward nowadays by the avant-garde. But many people will feel that such airy notions of religion are too thin to be worth bothering with. To take the discussion further, then, we must now consider the various kinds of impossibility that are involved when we are talking about our impossible loves.

(i) One has already been mentioned: it is the affinity between the impossible in logic and the forbidden in practical life. This is a complex and subtle issue, but we have to recall that during the first millennium BCE the fundamental concepts of philosophy were originally developed by partly secularizing and thus generalizing certain basic religious ideas. Thus what in a religious context was tabu or forbidden became in philosophy the impossible. The bridging idea, that "such a thing is unthinkable," is an interesting, paradoxical assertion—for how can I in plain language declare something unthinkable without thinking it? Even more striking, in archaic religious thought it is not only the unclean and the sinful that are forbidden, but the holy, the Sacred itself is also tabu or forbidden. And this suggests that the historical origins of the idea that God is impossible (wholly other, extra-ordinary, completely out of this world, utterly fearsome) may run a very long way back indeed.

Once we begin to enquire into the relation between the forbidden Sacred and the logically impossible, we notice that even while the former is giving birth to the latter, there remains a certain play between the two. A particularly interesting case is the one that arises when we ask whether the God of the Hebrew Bible is, like Eros in the Greek myth of Eros and Psyche, a god who can quite easily be seen but whom it is extremely dangerous and indeed forbidden to look at. Or is God simply an invisible Being who cannot possibly be seen by anyone, ever? Later orthodox monotheism says the latter: God is quite simply invisible. But the Old Testament very often seems to take the former view, and there are several occasions when living human beings do quite literally and with his permission "behold God." In Exodus 3:6 Moses is "afraid to look at God": he knows how dangerous it is. But in Exodus 24:9–11 God has no objection to being seen: he "did not lay his hand upon the chief men of the people of Israel: they beheld God, and ate and drank."[31]

The simplest solution to these puzzles is as follows: in the very earliest times the gods were seen as finite parts of the world, and were thought of as real and clearly visible beings. But Israel's chief leaders had a great sense of the awesome holiness of God, and they came to teach that it was extremely dangerous to look at God. You should hide your eyes, or veil your face, or look at God only from the rear. Alternatively, God might actually disarm himself and invite favoured individuals to feast with him. People who had ascended to Heaven in the sky might similarly be enabled to enjoy the "vision" of God after they were, in earthly terms, dead.

So far the account is reasonably clear. God is finite and anthropomorphic, and we are in a prescientific, pre-philosophical epoch in which the heavens are the sky and God normally lives up in the sky,[32] and sits enthroned upon the blue-glass skating rink of the Firmament. But the editors who finally put together the Hebrew Bible as we now have it were much influenced by Greek philosophy and therefore moving toward full philosophical monotheism, whose God is not in any way part of the world. God is transcendent, eternal, beyond the world, beyond language, and in no way anthropomorphic. He cannot be imaged at all. He is, quite simply, invisible. The posthumous vision of him will be intellectual, not optical. There cannot be a Jewish Acteon, who catches a glimpse of him. Thus it is no longer *forbidden* to see God, but simply impossible, and anyone who *looks* for God has failed to understand the word. And to protect the new account of God, the making of images of God is now prohibited.

As the new account of God became established, the world became "Nature," a law-governed material world relatively independent of God that could be studied by secular natural science. This radical and important shift helped to make our modern science-based culture possible. But what of God? In being entirely removed from the world and beyond language, God was now transcendent, wholly Other, invisible, ineffable, and relocated into a shadowy parallel universe that he shared with dead persons. Doesn't this imply that the leading religious thinkers were implicitly giving up "literal" or realistic belief in God just over two millennia ago? Had not God already become the Impossible God, non-realist and spectral, shortly before the birth of Christ? That would explain why the vivid personal God of Genesis and Exodus has faded so much as to become the notably inactive and mostly absent God of the New Testament. He is still invoked in flowery language, but he is not actually *doing* very much. To prove this thesis, all we would need is a demonstration that the main tradition of philosophical monotheism from Plato to Kant (including the Jewish and Islamic philosophers of the Middle Ages) never really justified its notion of degrees of being or reality, and therefore never justified its definition of God as *Ens realissimum*, the most-real Being. Hence the Great Tradition was always *ontologically* hollow (even if it didn't always know it) and the Impossible God was always the true God.

(ii) With that we turn to the second sense of the word "impossible"—the denotation of *logical* impossibility. Of the half-dozen kinds of impossible love that we are discussing, belief in God is the one which raises the questions of logical possibility most sharply, for if we cannot find a definition of God that is free from internal contradictions, then God cannot exist. And that is in fact the case: for the idea of God as generally understood in the West always attempts to combine the infinite, simple and timeless God of the philosophers with the finite, personal God of popular religion who is always seen as capable of having *dealings* with the believer. But a finite, quasi-personal being who is living, active, and communicative—even *language*-using—clearly cannot also be simple, infinite, and timeless. That which cannot change can neither talk nor otherwise respond!

Our tradition got itself into this fix because for such a long time there was no clear understanding of the Divine *infinity*. Once the full implications of philosophical theism were understood, the difficulty was obvious. Doctrines of "analogy" had to be developed and worked hard—*very* hard. Alternatively, Islam and some of the best Western minds (e.g., Erigena and Spinoza) tried to avoid the difficulty by developing an almost purely philosophical theism and playing down—or even eliminating—the mythical, anthropomorphic, and time-bound God of the popular tradition. But in the West it remains true that any account of God that can hope to be considered orthodox will be self-contradictory. It will try to conceive of God as living, active, and responsive (both personal and communicative) and at the same time as eternally utterly immobile—a patently absurd notion.

However, there have always been theologians of a more-or-less fideist persuasion who have moved in the opposite direction, and have even rejoiced in pointing out how contrary to reason much of Christian doctrine appears to be. The two most famous examples are Tertullian, who coined the phrase *Certum est quia impossibile* (it is certain because it is impossible), and Kierkegaard, who stresses very sharply the "Absolute Paradox" inherent in the orthodox dogma of the Incarnation when it asserts the union without confusion of two radically different natures in a single metaphysical subject.

One might ask at this point why someone as bright as Kierkeg-aard does not observe that the doctrine of God is *also* "absolutely paradoxical" in this sense. For in standard theology God has both eternal, metaphysical attributes such as simplicity, impossibility, aseity, etc., *and* such lowly time-bound human attributes as being alive, personal, loving, active, responsive, and so on. God already incorporates the Absolute Paradox in himself, and in his Incarna-tion in Christ he merely repeats it.

It is a desperate irony that Kierkegaard himself embodies the Absolute Paradox, for he tries to combine *in his own thought* the Platonism for which Real being has to be eternal with the post-Hegelian view that real being is always temporal. Poor man, he was caught up in paradox at three levels. And the vital question remains: If for figures like Tertullian and Kierkegaard the received tradition of Christian doctrine contained many paradoxes and gave rise to even more, why did they not conclude that Christian-ity cannot be true, and simply abandon it?

The likely orthodox reply is that from a higher point of view, namely God's, the Paradox does not arise. It all *looks* paradoxical, indeed; but only to us, because of our only-human and lower-world standpoint. All of this might be acceptable if a realist inter-pretation of belief in God were also acceptable. On a non-realist view it could be held that these highly paradoxical beliefs are so engaging that they will always return in "spectral" form. On both views it can also be pointed out that the paradox has an important disciplinary function: it involves a call to faith and to striving for transcendence. Religious symbols, understood non-realistically, may then be seen as focusing our various impossible loves. And we might add that the extreme paradoxicality of the dogma of the Incarnation has played a vital role in the education of the human race, because over the centuries it has acted as a bridge, helping Christianity to descend first into non-realist faith, and then into the final religion, which is Empty, radical, religious humanism. As we grasp successively that God is impossible; then that the Incar-nation is if anything even *more* so; and finally that any attempt to combine "real" extra-historical Absolutes with a fully historical outlook is always violently paradoxical, so we eventually come all the way down to earth and accept a religion of only-human immanence and secondariness. The Impossible has done its job by helping us to descend gradually from supernaturalism into the final truth, which is a simple acceptance of contingency.

(iii) The third kind of impossibility that deserves discussion here is practical impossibility, which is related to the fact that we live in time. During the course of your life it has often happened that an opportunity has suddenly presented itself and, disconcerted, you abruptly turned it down. Then the window of opportunity closed, for life moves on, relationships change, and everything is different. But in the meanwhile you have begun to have second thoughts. You would like to revisit that missed opportunity, and perhaps react to it differently. But there is no exact repetition: everything in life happens only once, and there are no retakes. In a certain sense, everything in our life instantly becomes irrevocable as soon as it passes. Every moment is a "last chance"; every *missed* opportunity turns quickly into a *lost* opportunity. And so it comes about that many of our impossible loves are simply lost opportunities that we are condemned to carry about with us for the rest of our lives—possible partners we might have had, possible selves we might have become, possible allegiances that we might have embraced.

A consequence of all this is that we moderns are acutely aware that the life that has turned out to be ours is only one of an indefinitely large number of possible lives that we might have had if only we had reacted otherwise at various turning-points. I haven't really got anyone else to blame for the way things have turned out; like everyone else, I've had my chances.

What are we doing, then, when we brood over these other lives and other selves that might have been ours? We are thinking about the limits of life, about how small and narrow the actual course of things is compared with the illimitable expanse of the possible that stretches away on either side of it—and also thinking that we'll never be able to see the whole course of our life as making sense, because even if we do still endorse quite large tracts of our life when we did steer a straight course, there will remain many turning-points when we were taken by surprise and acted unthinkingly and foolishly. So if I am to reach a moment at the end of my life when I do feel able to say "Amen" to life in general and to my own actual life in particular, then I will have to be ready to include in my "Amen" an acceptance of all my own lost opportunities, misjudgments and mistakes. If I brood over them, then, it is because they are part of the record, and I need to find a way of accepting them as striking illustrations of the general contingency of life.

Aimless Love

I have another kind of impossible love to describe. Because it has no biologically determined aim or function, but is quite gratuitous and even irrational, normal people may well regard it as "supernatural" and probably impossible. Since it is no doubt disputable, and may never have been described before, this seems the appropriate place for it, immediately after the ideas introduced in the previous chapter and apart from the topics discussed in the preceding catalogue of Impossible Loves. I include it because if my description is recognized by at least a few other people, we may be stumbling upon something newly emerging that will in due course become of great religious importance.

Of all human loves, the two most important are the child/parent bond and heterosexual love. Both are of course biologically driven. The bond with the mother is usually established within days of birth. There used to be a ritual enactment of the bonding with the father: he being seated, the baby was placed on his knees or, more accurately, in his lap—that which is "in his lap" being what he will take responsibility for, protect, and care for. Next followed a moment of indecision, during which the baby's fate was "in the lap of the gods". Then, if all was well, the father would not reject the child but accept it as truly his, and the bond was established.

The parental bond, once established, is prodigiously strong—so strong that even a child who is badly abused at home will commonly deny everything in order not to be separated from its parents. To be sure, a certain "leaving" of one's parents occurs at marriage, but whereas marriage is conventionally terminated by death, when parents die they return in startling strength. For nearly all of us, our parents are—or will in due course become—the most important of our dead.

The next most important of our loves is "straight" heterosexual love, the "love" here being a huge cultural elaboration of a biological mechanism, namely sexual object-choice. The first of two obvious points about heterosexual love that need to be stressed here is that love is (initially, at least) strictly for the sake of sex. Especially for the young, the language of love is the language of *courtship*. If you (being a man) tell a young woman that you love her, she will understand you to be saying that she is your chosen sexual object, and that you are quite ready and willing to go through at least some of the conventional preliminaries to sex. She instantly understands this, takes it entirely seriously, and settles down to the very agreeable business of consulting her feelings and negotiating terms. Highly complex calculations and delicate questionings follow. But if you were to say, "I love you—but I'm offering you *only* love, and not love for the sake of sex," she will be at first baffled and then highly suspicious. What is he talking about? What's his game? The whole world knows that heterosexual love is not for its own sake, but primarily for the sake of something bigger and more important, namely sex.

The second point is that in heterosexual love much emphasis lies on the fact that your chosen object is of the *opposite* sex, *really* opposite. The otherness of the other is the point, and it entails elements of suspicion, antipathy, and conflict that are highly amusing and extremely exciting. Indeed, this otherness is the point of the whole business. It makes the negotiations interesting. It gives to sex a dialectical and even a certain *cosmological* significance, one that in our post-metaphysical times no other sort of love has any longer.[33]

Another kind of love to be discussed is different for the two sexes. For men it is the feeling one has for one's closest colleagues, comrades-in-arms, teammates, shipmates—the fellowmen with whom one has shared a common allegiance and faced a common peril, or a great task. This is the male bond that may fade with changing times, but that often remains strong enough for men to be keen to go on attending reunions for the rest of their lives.

The female counterpart of this is the Best Friend. Because a woman even yet has to live so much more on her guard than a man, and has to be very careful about just how far and how explicitly she commits herself, she needs a confidante, a second self, someone she can trust and with whom she can be completely unguarded as she discusses her current feelings and the state of her negotiations with Men.

These extra-close friendships with a comrade or a confidante should perhaps also be considered as biologically conditioned. Most young adult humans are most at their ease in the company of their own sex, and the examples cited are the strongest cases of really *important* same-sex friendship. Yet as everyone knows, they both have to give way to serious heterosexual love. Serious sexual love is often more important than religion or nationality, either of which can be changed for its sake; and usually more important than even the closest comradeship or the most intimate Best Friendship. Serious sex creates an overriding bond.

Against this background, aimless love is a kind of love that seems to lack both biological conditioning and a sexual aim. It may be felt for someone of either sex. Impelled by this extremely strong affection or liking, one rings other persons up, checks up on them, looks out for them, and strongly desires to see them frequently. It is a strange, specially heightened form of friendship. The person for whom I feel this kind of love is not "opposite," even if a woman, but is someone with whom I identify. Perhaps I see in her an image of my own younger self; or perhaps he is for me an image of one of the selves I might have become but didn't. I don't know, it's hard to say: but one is aware of a bond something like what might exist with one's twin, or perhaps an *alter ego*. One dare not be too explicit in communicating this sort of thing, because if the other does not fully reciprocate, then too open an avowal might cause uneasiness and even end the friendship. But in some cases at least, a clear degree of reciprocation exists: the other does get the point.

Most often, I suppose, aimless love is left undeclared, and many people will feel that it is all the sweeter for remaining permanently unspoken. It does not need to declare itself, because it does not need to win the other's consent and co-operation—and sometimes it may be entirely unconscious. Think of the idiom that we sometimes use to make someone aware of it in retrospect: **"Didn't you know that he's been carrying a torch for you all these years?"** It reminds us of how delicate are the degrees of consciousness in these matters, not only within the individual, but also between people.

Human loves are not always entirely "pure," of course, and it may easily happen that some erotic strands enter into a man's "aimless" love for a woman. But it still remains quite different from true heterosexual love because it lacks the tension between *opposites* that is characteristic of heterosexual love. In the past, when the sexes lived rather more segregated lives, men and women seldom met without being acutely aware of this tension. Aimless love between a man and a woman was probably unknown. The very thought of it would have seemed baffling. But in today's more relaxed climate it has become possible, and even common.

What about the possibility in former times of aimless love between two persons of the same sex? Gay historians have recently been pointing out a number of cases within the Christian tradition—some historical, some mythical—of this sort of intimate alliance between men. The paired names are familiar: David and Jonathan, Jesus and the Beloved Disciple, Paul and Barnabas, Cosmas and Damian, Cyril and Methodius, and so on. These pairs are sometimes said to have been gay, but lacking any definite evidence either way, we could as well imagine them aimless lovers of the sort I describe. The same may be true of many "special friendships" in religious communities.

For how many people might one feel in this way? I'd guess two or three. Perhaps a few more, or in some cases perhaps only one. And the aimless love may go on being important for many decades: certainly as many as four.

I have already hinted at why I think aimless love may be religiously significant. In being "aimless" and yet surprisingly intense, it resembles our love of life and love of the world. Perhaps it is the counterpart of these loves in the world of human relationships. And something else needs to be added. We late-moderns are acutely aware of all the other selves we might have become, other lives we might have lived, and so on. Perhaps in our aimless loves we are pursuing a synthesis—seeking a wider spiritual self-realization for ourselves, and seeking it in and through loving other people with whom we identify. This would be a postmodern version of the old Kant-and-Hegel attempt to find a language in which we can integrate the individual quest for the good with the social pursuit of a *common* good.

If so, then aimless love may indeed have no biologically prescribed aim, but rather a religious one.[34] We may not be capable of true *agape,* but certainly we can experience *philia* as well as *eros.*

10

That's the Story of My Life

S ince early times people have been narrating life stories and wondering what kind of story the story of a whole human life is—or can be made into. Where have we come from, and where are we going? Is the entire plot predestined, or is up to us to invent the "meaning"? Is the whole best seen as tragedy, or as comedy? Are we moving towards a known destination, or are we seekers?

Life as a journey

Until the Bronze Age began, most human beings lived a wandering life as hunter-gathers or pastoralists, and until mechanized transport became readily available travel was very slow. It is not surprising that when our ancestors sought an understanding of human life as a whole, they very commonly did so by telling the story of a man's life as the story of a great journey. In this life we are *in via*, on the way; and the image of the journey is so pervasive that even to this day it underlines the way we usually frame many of our questions about life: Where have we come from? Where are we going? Has our journey been planned in advance for us? Have we a written itinerary to guide us? Are we pilgrims, heading along a well-worn Way to a definite destination? Or are we seekers, on a quest and hoping we will recognize what we're looking for if and when we bump into it? Alternatively, might we be content like Abraham to find our fulfilment along the way? We travel, we have various adventures, we survive, we remain true to our God and we survive being more than once tested *by* him. We become established, we see our children grow, we watch our descendants multiply, and we die peacefully. Is that not the best life story for a man of faith? What more could one wish for than a life like Abraham's?

We take it for granted that the major figures of the Bible were all of them travellers; but they were not quite content with Abraham's conception of life's journey. Moses the prophet and lawgiver leads a mass migration of his whole people to their promised land; Elijah and Jesus are portrayed as wandering prophets and healers; and Paul is an itinerant evangelist who plants and nurtures his own little circuit of congregations. All four have a task in life, a special mission to be accomplished.

Outside the Biblical tradition, Odysseus' great journey is simply his oft-interrupted trip home—as if one of life's greatest tasks is the task of simply coming full circle and *recollecting* oneself. Three other figures who are very congenial to us moderns are Gilgamesh, Mahavira and the Buddha. They travel in search of an answer to the question of life's limits: passing and passing away, chance, suffering, and death. Can we conquer life's limits, or escape them, or must we find some way of coming to terms with them? Gilgamesh fails to find the immortality he seeks. By severe asceticism and much meditation Mahavira eventually achieves a total understanding of things, *kevala jnana*, in which he finds bliss. The Buddha follows a similar path, and formulates a carefully worked out therapy for human unhappiness. Both of the latter two figures think that it is possible in this life to enjoy an anticipation of the final illumination and beatitude that is the goal of life. This idea survives in Christian doctrine to this day: the goal of life is the vision of God in heaven, and the saint is a person who even in this life has enjoyed a foretaste of it.

Life as an ascent

Rather than the Buddha, it was Mahavira, the legendary founder of the Jain religion, who first taught that we should see our life as the ascent of a mountain, an upward climb through a series of degrees of knowledge or stages of cognition. With the help of ascetical practices, meditation, and education, the believer gradually purifies his mind and comes to see everything more clearly. As this concept was repeated and elaborated in many traditions, it commonly pictured three main stages in the ascent: from a merely sense-based, empirical kind of knowledge, the student rose first to discursive understanding (understanding in terms of general ideas and laws, and explanatory theories), and finally to purely intuitive or immediate insight—a pure intellectual vision of the whole as it is, and a full understanding of why everything is, and must eternally be just as it is. In this vision we find a total and timeless satisfaction.

In the West it was above all Plato who established a version of these ideas which remained prominent in the philosophical tradition until Hegel, and in the religious tradition until today (or perhaps until yesterday). But in East and West, the core ideas are strikingly similar: a human life is best spent in the pursuit of a special blessedness-bestowing or divine kind of knowledge, a total visionary understanding of what eternally is and must be. To attain this enlightenment we need progressively to purify ourselves and train ourselves to meditate on higher things, so that we ascend through a series of stages of knowledge. And when we reach the top, we are supremely and eternally blessed in the knowledge that we are now securely established in the spiritual world. We will be finally freed from evil and sin—or, alternatively, from the fate of having to undergo rebirth.

Stages on life's way

Long ago, Aristotle and his followers arranged all living organisms in a vertical order of rank, commonly called the Ladder of Nature (*scala naturae*), with the lowest-ranking creatures at the bottom, and the highest at the top. But then in the nineteenth century the new development-minded thinkers had the bright idea of tipping the ladder over and forwards in time, so that it became an historical sequence of stages of development.[35] The vertical sequence of the rock strata had already come to be seen as the source materials for writing an historical science of geology, and the sequence of the fossils in the same rocks now similarly provided evidence for an historical science of biology.

It was simple and brilliant, and in the age of Hegel and Kierkegaard the same thing was done with the religious life. After metaphysics, people were much less inclined to see the human self as a timeless, immortal, spiritual substance called "the soul." Instead, the self was coming to be seen in terms of psychology and biography: I am my own unfolding life in time, I am continuously developing in a way that conducts me through a series of profoundly different understandings of myself and my world. In this way the old stages in the ascent of the mind to God come to be seen as stages in personal development.

Thus with Hegel and Kierkegaard a much stronger sense of history—both of the history of ideas in society generally, and of the human self as developing throughout its own life—has in effect tipped the old platonic ladder of spirituality forwards in time, making it into the starting-point for a new vision of every human life as involved in a personal religious journey. Everyone nowadays is a pilgrim, everyone is conscious of having passed through a series of stages of intellectual and religious development. What is more, after Hegel and Kierkegaard it is destined to become obvious to all that there is no longer any one ultimate, ready-made, ruling Truth of things. Truth itself is becoming plural: thus in Kierkegaard's *Stages on Life's Way* (1845) each of the stages or spheres of existence is a more or less complete and autonomous vision of life. The three stages are in effect three distinct worlds.[36]

Yet neither Hegel nor Kierkegaard drew the obvious conclusion that when our thinking has become fully historical we must abandon all ideas of a final, consummating, history-ending revelation of Truth at the end of the line. They both arranged their series of stages with the "highest" coming last. Darwin was well aware of the danger of portraying the history of life on earth as a story of an "advance" from "lower" to "higher" life forms. Hegel and Kierkegaard failed to draw the analogous conclusion that it is a mistake to portray human spiritual life as a single-track journey in one direction, namely from "lower" to "higher" stations along the line. They try to show that the life of the spirit is dialectical: that at each of the "lower" stages various difficulties, stresses, and contradictions arise, and do so to a degree that eventually forces the individual to jump to the next "higher" level. But they both neglect to describe situations of the same kind that sometimes force one to jump *in the opposite direction.*

You want an autobiographical example? I am an unusually visual person, for whom great painting and architecture often trigger profound religious experiences. In Buddhist mood, I like the way visual art can liberate and "decenter" or dissolve the anxious self, finding in such visual joy an image—indeed, an actual *experience*—of salvation. So I hate the way that ascetical "ladder spiritualities" always rank the senses at the very bottom of the scale. Given a choice, I'd always prefer to look at a good Matisse rather than indulge in purely rational contemplation of the abstract Form of Beauty. And that is why I can well imagine myself often wanting to move in the opposite direction, *down* the line, from purely spiritual to purely sensual experience.[37]

Life as a journey on the Metro

These considerations force one finally to abandon the conception
of the religious life as a single-track and one-way upwards journey
in a mountain railway train, with stations at the bottom, at various
mid-levels (the Hong Kong term: see the Peak Tramway there),
and finally at the summit. Instead, we adopt the model of a metro
map. It is multitrack, and you can travel in *either* direction; but
note that the map does preserve the suggestion that the ordering
of the stations is not wholly arbitrary. On the contrary, there are
often obvious links between neighboring stations. (And by the
way, the reader may recall the delightful fact that the mass transit
system of Athens today is called the *Metaphorai*, "the carry-over."
Metaphor carries meaning across time and space, as life's railway
carries us seekers after meaning).

I attempted an account of the spiritual life along these lines in
Life Lines (1986). I stuck to the idea that the stages on the way are
many different intellectual and religious positions or standpoints
or outlooks, and arranged sixteen of them on a multitrack Me-
tromap. The first idea for the book was that it would be written as
a video game, by playing which you could find yourself and your
own journey in life. But I was fated never to become sufficiently
computer-literate, and in any case such a video game would have
been far too serious to be bought by modern people. Who in his
right mind would want to find *himself*? And who wants to know
where she's heading in life? It is only too usual nowadays to go a
whole lifetime without ever encountering anyone who is serious
about religion, either in the churches or anywhere else. My video
game would never find any market.

So the video game was out of the question, and a book it had to
be. But a book is unilinear, and a book has a beginning and an end.
I could hardly avoid writing the book as a journey from childhood
towards death in successive chapters, a format that inevitably and
despite my map gave its (very few) readers the impression that I
was still prescribing a one-way journey from "lower" to "higher"
positions or levels of truth.

Solar living

Ten years later I had another go at the idea in *Solar Ethics* (1995).
If there is no one great Truth for all of us waiting out there, and if
therefore all systems of truth are humanly created and projected
outward so that all our life stories are our own fictions, then only

one way is left to find the Pearl of Great Price, the thing that the religious seeker is looking for. We must create and find it for ourselves by committing ourselves one hundred per cent to life in the present moment. Give up the idea of "saving your soul," because you haven't got one. Instead, conquer your own fear of death and give yourself completely to life, and then live by "passing away" all the time. You are a mortal, and therefore you should live a dying life.

In putting forward this idea I relied upon modern people's evident need to seek to purify themselves by self-expression. For us late moderns, **coming out** is the best way of **coming clean**—a very neat pair of idioms. And I also relied upon everyone's experience of how redemptive it is to "lose oneself" in love or in creative work.

On the whole, I cannot complain. The idea of solar living was quite indulgently received. But people naturally—and rightly— took me to be saying that this one very intense and thin idea was the only way left for us to talk about the religious life. Friends said, "I'm trying to stop being 'tight' and start being solar," and that was fine so far as it went. I said, "The test will come when the medical people announce to us our imminent death. Can we go all the way into death in a state of solar joy? We should, indeed we must do that: it's the only conquest of death." But that was about as far as it got. In the face of modern nihilism I had felt compelled to pin everything on this one intense, burning idea. When you are dying, it may be very good for you; but if you are still in the middle of life, it is likely too thin.[38]

Aware of this, I settled for a few years upon a slightly different formula: solar personal ethics, humanitarian social ethics. Much of what passes for morality and moral conviction in the contemporary world strikes me as highly unattractive, but the thoroughgoing humanitarian ethic of the peacekeeper and the "aid worker" seems a wholesome and fitting model by which to live one's life. So for a while I rested on that simple formula.

More recently, I have seen a way of enriching the solar living formula to include the religious life. Arising from the "everyday speech" books of 1999/2000, it recognizes modern people as being already highly demythologized. They have experienced what we have elsewhere been calling the Return of the Great Questions.[39] They are highly aware of the limits of life as we now—in view of the end of supernatural belief and metaphysics—see them afresh. Temporality, contingency, finitude: Time, Chance and Death.

We might see the modern religious quest as being for each of us our personal attempt to understand and come to terms with the limits of life. In his last major interview, Jacques Derrida put it like this: "At last (*enfin*) to learn how to live—and how to die. How to die—and how to live, maybe."[40] It takes us a long time—indeed, it may take a lifetime—to learn to recognize the limits of life, to learn how to negotiate them, to learn how to accept them, and to understand that living and dying make up a single package to which each of us must learn to say his own Amen.

On this account, "solar living" remains the best slogan or description for the *active* religious life, and "cosmic emotion" remains the best description for the *contemplative* aspect of the religious life.[41] But I can now see how to develop this account further, and that is by giving much more attention to our long, complicated battles with the limits of life. In *The Great Questions of Life* I deal with that topic from one angle, and in this present book we have found another angle by asking ourselves why it is that we spend so much of our lives worrying about and chasing after so many kinds of unattainable, impossible, paradoxical objects of love. So far, we have suggested an answer: We are bumping up against the limits of life, dreaming the impossible dream of being able to transcend them, trying to understand them, and trying in particular to understand the fact that our personal lifetimes span different periods, and often cause us to become eternally and impossibly separated from each other.

11

Sweet Sorrow

A mbivalent feelings have long been prominent in religion. In the Hebrew Bible, God has strongly ambivalent feelings about Israel: his justice is in conflict with his maternal compassion for his errant child.[42] Israel similarly has strongly ambivalent feelings about God: he is the one who strives with God, rebelling like an awkward adolescent against a love that is far too great and too demanding for human beings to bear. And indeed, long before Freud, theologians and religious writers recognized the extent to which the man-God relation is bedevilled by value conflicts: justice versus mercy, Law versus Gospel, rational order versus spontaneity and freedom. Usually it is suggested that the conflict arises from the extreme disproportion, the infinite qualitative difference, between the two parties in what should be a relationship of *love*. God's infinite power and knowledge and, in particular, his *eternity* cannot but make any attempt by a human being to live out a settled love-relationship with God run into paradoxes. For example, God, being eternal and omniscient, cannot even *recognize* the conflict between the duty to keep all the rules, and the yearning for free, creative self-expression. Why? Because the conflict can arise only for a being that lives in time. How could *God* distinguish between long-term and short-term considerations? God knows no distinction between long and short, nor between near and far. For him there is only here, only

---

The title of this chapter is from *Romeo and Juliet* II.ii.184. Juliet recognizes that love wishes to cling to its object, but acknowledges that it must not do so, for "I should kill thee with much cherishing."

now. But insofar as these contrasts do shape *my* moral experience, I am bound to run into problems in my relationship with God.

For a parallel, consider the feminist revolt in the middle and later years of the nineteenth century. In the micropolitics of human relationships, patriarchy still ruled. It very often happened that a woman of scarcely more than twenty years found herself newly married to a man who was in early middle age and professionally established. He was relatively rich and powerful, and well able to protect and support her. In fact he was often so loving and indulgent, so wise and kind, that she need only gratefully accept his rule. The Father-knows-best vision of the world reigned seemingly unchallenged, to such a degree that she could continue indefinitely being his pet, his pampered child, and it was quite unnecessary for her ever to grow up. But their inequality was stifling: she found his protective paternal wisdom and love unendurable and rebelled at the prospect of perpetual childhood. For his part, he found her discontent utterly incomprehensible: he had done everything for her, and truly loved and cared for her, and she lacked nothing; so what on earth could she be complaining about?

In the later years of the eighteenth century a similar discontent began to affect the man-God relationship. People's overall vision of the world was becoming more centered around the human subject. In the philosophy of Kant it was beginning to be understood that we build our own knowledge, that we build our own vision of the world, that we freely recognize the main principles of a rational morality and impose them upon ourselves, and finally that it is we the people who give to our elected political leaders their authority over us. In short, as Kant puts it, human beings were increasingly coming of age and taking charge of their own affairs. The old image of a loving Father-God who lays everything on for us and surrounds us with total care and protection—asking in return only the absolute minimum, namely unconditional acceptance of his rule—that whole image had become obsolete and inappropriate. We humans now have to assume full adult responsibility for our knowledge, our morality, and our politics. We want to be able to change things: since it was *we* who created the present set-up, why can't we modify it?

What is then to happen to God? One view, found in Kant himself and in many successors (including, at one time, the present writer), is that God may live on, provided that he gives up all his power—which in effect means, his objective existence—and becomes simply a guiding spiritual ideal, a symbol of love. Within a century, however, this "non-realist" view of God was being edged aside. As Friedrich Nietzsche put it, "the old God has died, and Kant's God is merely his ghost." God now has the same status as the dead parents who are enthroned in our imaginations—non-existent, eternal, benign, venerated, and utterly inactive.

In effect, Nietzsche showed that there is no half-way house: the non-realist God is a dead God, still loved and revered, still influential in some degree and still prayed to—but inactive and dead.

However, if you think that is the end of the story you have got another think coming, for the relation to God goes on. We continue to have strong, ambivalent feelings about God. . . . No, it's worse than that, because many or most of our impossible loves continue to trouble us and continue to generate strong ambivalent feelings in us.

Why? Because, just as someone may go on being in love with a dead spouse, so we commonly remain deeply attached to our old and now-thoroughly-exploded religious ideas. And also because we are still torn all the time between a need to rebel against the limits of life, to try to find some way round them, and a need simply to calm down and accept them. We are irritatingly, chronically, fretful and discontented: we find it no easier to live without an objective god than it was to live with him. We try to hold on to such remnants of God's world as the belief in an objective rational order "out there," objective Truth, and objective moral standards. Odd that all those enlightenment realists about knowledge and values firmly remain closet theists even though they like to assure the world that they are "atheists." They aren't: they are still as attached to God as anyone.

Have you considered that the reason you love your parents and think of them *more* now that they are dead is that you can no longer quarrel with them and get irritated by them? They just sit "up there, looking down" upon you, benign and silent. You even talk to them, sometimes. Certainly you feel that they continue to be around, somehow propping your world up and holding it all together as they did when you were young. And so it is with God: a vague cultural memory of God is still enthroned in your imagination, and is still propping up the objective reality of things, still grounding objective Truth, and still underpinning objective value—at least, that's how it was for the realist philosopher Bernard Williams. All of which shows what we human beings still are, even in the twenty-first century. Each of us is split between a desire to grow up and assume full responsibility for our world and our values, and a contrary impulse to keep God around as a sea anchor, a fail-safe mechanism, a back-up in case things go badly wrong with us. We keep God "just in case" exactly as your children, twenty years after they left home, still require their old bedrooms to be kept up in the family home "just in case." As yet only a few "nihilists" and "relativists" amongst us are ready to try to live entirely without God, without even the ghost of God. We can as yet scarcely begin to imagine what form the religious life might take in a world of signs with no fixed points.

Similar conflicting feelings trouble our other impossible loves, the ones that yearn after impossibly pure ideals, and the ones that ask more of human love than it can deliver. You try for "great" love as if you did not know in your heart that it is an impossible dream; and you give your wife an eternity ring and say you'll love her "forever," as if you did not know perfectly well that all too soon one of you will die, leaving the other to wait to follow, for you both know that neither of you will wish to live for long without the other. People say casually that they will "always" do this, and will remember that "forever," but we all know that there *is* no "always" or "forever" in human affairs. As for all our accessible and unattainable loves, we had best simply put them down to the mischievousness of Eros. He loves to make fools of us.

Nevertheless, a dim background recognition of the radical, all-the-way-down contingency and insecurity of life is common to us all now. It colors all our loves with a touch of anguish, making them bittersweet, or at least poignant. "Look thy last on all things lovely / Every hour," because they are all passing away, and so are you—at the same speed. I want to argue that the mark of religious truth today is that one is ready honestly to acknowledge the ubiquity of this bittersweet anguish, even in our most joyful and world-affirming moods. The difficulty is in accepting it—for there is no gain without loss, no joy without that pang at one's heart—and the problem is how to distill that anguish and make it sweet, so that we can say "Yes" to it, too.

12

Religion after the West

A t the very beginning of the nineteenth century, Hegel introduced into Western thought the notion that the entire Western cultural tradition was coming to completion. He described a vast synthesis that united Plato's ascent, through a series of stages of knowledge and up to a total vision of the Good, with the old Judeo-Christian vision of divine Providence orchestrating all human history towards a grand climax, the ultimate happy ending. Versions of this optimistic story about the end of the Western tradition were put forward by several subsequent thinkers, including Karl Marx. But in the later years of the century the mood darkened, and the End as consummation was replaced by the end as disintegration and termination. The received Enlightenment optimism about reason, progress, and human perfectibility had overreached itself, and began to break down. Nietzsche announced the coming of nihilism, and Oswald Spengler prophesied *The Decline of the West*.[43]

The history of the West during the twentieth century has largely confirmed these fears, as catastrophic wars and political upheavals rapidly ended Europe's nearly four centuries of world leadership. Spiritually, the West had rested on an alliance of Greek metaphysical philosophy and Judeo-Christian religion, but by the end of the twentieth century Europe had disowned both. Even in Europe the old European civilization was replaced by the new and very different American consumerism, and America itself now paid no more than lip service to what it had inherited from the old Europe. This is not surprising, for as the current rip-roaring development in East Asia shows, the new capitalist-consumerist culture is independent of the old West and does not need its values. If intelligently managed and led, it can and does flourish anywhere. It does not need philosophy, it does not need religion: all it really needs is *technology*, and the rest is no more than decoration. And as for the human spirit . . . whatever was that? Nobody can remember any longer. In consumer society an inclination to serious philosophical and religious thought is merely an indication of trouble with one's serotonin levels, and is soon put right by appropriate medication. For a true consumerist, we now know, it is not just that God is dead and that the real world is dead, but that thought, serious thought, is dead too.

Within the old Europe, we find it hard to avoid the feeling that we have nowhere left to go—except perhaps towards the "black" and post-historical kind of art that is our version of Dada and Surrealism, or towards Buddhism. This pessimism is only confirmed by the way our last great philosophers seem always to have ended up stuck inside their own systems of thought, leaving their followers not quite knowing where they should go next. This is true of Heidegger, Wittgenstein and Derrida. When you have fully absorbed their final messages, what next?

Is there any possibility of reconstructing or renewing the Western tradition? Nietzsche—still perhaps the greatest of the modern philosophers, and not yet eclipsed by his successors—foresaw the need for reconstruction, but is rather vague and airily uplifting when the time for making concrete proposals comes round. A new kind of human being will have the strength to create new gods, new myths, and new values. Heidegger does a little better when he takes up another Nietzschean theme: he suggests that Western thought must now return into its own origins and confront again the question of Being as it was confronted by the first Western philosophers. I have tried to develop this theme by talking of the way that the end of dogmatic metaphysics and that of dogmatic religious belief have effectively stripped us naked, so that we are defenseless in the face of the contingency of existence and have experienced in very intense form "the Return of the Great Questions." I'm saying, in effect, that the end of dogmatic metaphysical philosophy, historical criticism of our great religious traditions, and our contemporary craze for technology and consumerism have between them effectively wiped out our inherited religious traditions. Almost nothing of any value is left. It is now too late for reconstruction, and too late for any salvage operations. We should let the dead bury their dead, and get on with the task of reinventing religion *ex nihilo*—starting from nothing, beginning from scratch.

Why? And *how?*—if, as I have suggested, postmodern consumer society has successfully eliminated any felt need for philosophical and religious foundations by regarding them as the expression of a mood disorder. In postmodern entertainment culture people live absorbed in contemplating the "mediascape"—the rich, complex, imaginary world projected for their distraction by the mass media.[44] The mediascape is like a vast soap opera—beginningless, endless, rambling in all directions, and filling the whole of cultural space. It is totalitarian: it is a box that hardly anybody has the strength to think outside of. Like a black hole, it swallows everything. I have no answer to it, only an obstinate conviction that there must be more to life than this. Even the people who are most hypnotized by the mediascape must surely know in their hearts that human beings can do better than this wretched opium dream.

I persist, therefore, in saying that after the end of the old West and of all the other major cultural traditions, we need to think about reconstructing the whole of humanity's ideal culture.[45] To begin with, we must go back into the original nakedness and emptiness, and move step-by-step. We need to establish a minimal notion of what the world is and what our place in it is, and we also need to show how human animals can learn to bear the knowledge of what they are and where they stand, and then be reconciled to their own lives.

We have to start, I propose, with a minimal conception of the facts of life, of what it is to be human in a human world. We have to learn how to live and die with a knowledge of our own contingency and transcience that other animals do not have to bear. In this sense, and in spite of everything, I still believe that philosophical and religious thinking has a certain logical priority. It alone provides the platform on which a sane and healthy cultural ideal can be built. (If you disagree, then you probably deem it no longer possible to get any leverage against technology and the mediascape, and you should therefore throw this book away at once.)

So we begin. As I have suggested, we begin with the simplest and clearest possible *worldview.* It recognizes only two entities: life in general, and my life. Life is the general ongoing flow of events and of symbolic exchange in the human social world. My life is my own personal role in it all.[46]

Against that background, we next define *religion*. Religion, I suggest, is the complex of ideas and practices by means of which we try to reconcile ourselves to, and make the best of, life in general and our own lives in particular. Religion is about coming to terms with life: that is, learning how to live and how to die.

Why do we need to be reconciled to life? Because our life is subject to certain permanent *limits*, of which we (unlike other animals) are highly aware, for our language teaches us about them. These limits are mutually implicated with each other, and are so deeply a part of our experience that we cannot really imagine life without them; but they cause us to fret a great deal, and we keep looking for ways round them. They are time, chance, and death— or in traditional philosophical language, temporality, contingency, and finitude. Life is always subject to *temporality*, in such a way that nothing is ever done or enjoyed or achieved totally and simultaneously. We do or enjoy everything only in a chain of succeeding stages, a bit at a time. Life is a one-way journey: it allows (as everyone knows) for no retakes and no return tickets. Life is always subject to *contingency*, and (despite what the insurance industry says) there is no guaranteed protection against the disasters that may strike any of us at any time. We have to try hard to take full control of our own lives, even as we know that we can never entirely succeed. Fortune holds the aces. And life is always subject to *finitude*, in that it will never yield to us the endless and unalloyed perfection we dream of, and it is always terminated by death.

We have just emerged from a cultural epoch that has lasted nearly three thousand years, since the beginning of the Iron Age. It was a period in which great religious belief systems and philosophies, very widely diffused, were developed to protect people from too naked a view of the contingency of human existence and the nothingness of death. But in recent years those painted veils have crumbled away, bringing about a return of philosophy's primal terrors. Many people now find that their personal happiness in life is permanently ruined by the nagging, inescapable, unanswerable terror of the great questions that prey upon their minds. That is why religion is so much needed: it helps to pilot us through the terrors, and helps us to find personal happiness and fulfilment in life in the face of those unanswerable Questions.

In short, this means that whereas the older kind of religion was often about salvation from sin, the chief interest of modern religion is in learning how to live with nihilism. Rather than the "conquest" of nihilism—a romantic cliché—life today calls for

familiarization with nihilism—the acceptance of the radical contingency of everything.

At this point we should also briefly refer to the distinction
between *organized religion* and *spirituality*. Organized religion
is large-scale, traditional, and authoritative, in the manner of the
world faiths with which we are familiar. It situates a large community within a grand narrative vision of world history. A spirituality,
on the other hand, is a religious style that someone has personally
worked out for herself. Today, when the old world faiths are dying
and many people are finding themselves suddenly stranded by the
rapid decay of their traditions, a good deal of spirituality has per-
force sprung up. But it is very difficult indeed to face these great
questions on one's own, and very difficult to frame any kind of
rational response to them for oneself. We still need conversations
with others to stabilize our vocabulary and to maintain our sanity. Therefore, the religion of the future will need to have a social
dimension so that it can develop a clear and publicly intelligible
vocabulary.

We next need to spell out in a little more detail how religion
may help us to come to terms with the great questions of life.

Many people, I know, will think it impossible. They'll say that
we humans are like a line of rather nervous beasts walking into an
abattoir. Suddenly a heavy rubber curtain parts, and their nos-
trils twitch as they get an unmistakeable whiff of what is coming.
They go into a desperate screaming panic, but it's too late, for the
slaughterman's bolt hits the back of the skull and it's all over. The
people I have in mind will tell you that the whole of our human
life is compressed into that final stage of animal life, the second
or two between the moment of realization of what's coming, and
the end. As described by Pascal, Nietzsche, and others, that is the
human condition: to live all your life knowing what pigs and cattle
recognize only in the last few seconds of their lives. What possible
remedy can there be for that?

My answer is threefold. First, we should not attempt to escape
from the terrors of existence. Instead, we should by faith cast
ourselves into existence in all its one-way temporality, its contingency, and its transience. We must both recognize clearly what
our life is, and find the courage for the *solar* living that nevertheless says "Yes" to life, and steps boldly out over the abyss.

In the second place, we will of course often find ourselves
flooded by anxiety and terror; but it is a psychological fact that
the passions are easily deflected, and easily revalued. How readily

we eroticize the things of which we are most afraid! Still more striking is religion's uncanny power not only to allow overwhelming feelings of dread, anxiety, and terror to overflow, decentring the self and freeing us from self-concern; but also to revalue these same vast feelings and turn them into *cosmic emotion*—ethereal feelings of exaltation, awe, bliss, and peace. Thus a man who is dying is not obliged to go kicking and screaming into his own final extinction. He can if he chooses make of his own dying a blissful, mystical drowning in God, and so revalue his own extinction even as he slips into it.

And in the third place, I propose that a new and thoroughly post-Western reconstruction of culture will not dream of attempting to escape or transcend the facts of life. There is no transcendent or supernatural order. We *are* our own lives in all their temporality, contingency and finitude, and there is no supernatural or transcendent realm. We reject medieval religion's painted screen, and we reject modern technology's mediascape. Instead, we'll try for a culture that is not built on illusions, but is truthful, honest, and open all the way down.

What does a solar religious life look like? First, it involves an attempt to *find your own voice*—that is, to find the lifestyle through which you can best and most fully express yourself. Second, you must attempt to *appropriate your own life* and assume full responsibility for it. Third, your personal living should be as affirmative and extravertive as you can make it: *each of us should so act as to enhance and increase the overall value of life.*

It is worth commenting here that all the greatest moral advances of the past seventy years have been of this type: feminism strives to raise the general social valuation of females; environmentalism strives to raise our valuation of our physical environment and of all the living things that populate it; anti-racism and the many movements descended from it strive to raise our valuation of racial groups other than our own; and finally, humanitarian ethics responds simply to human need, without regard to any calculation of the relative merits of individuals.

If we are still able to be hopeful about human beings and the human future, it is largely on the basis of what these four great movements have already done to make the human world a better place today than it was in earlier periods. That is why I argue that as an absolutely minimal basis for ethics in the future, we should learn to love life and to try to live as affirmatively as we can, acting always to raise rather than to lower the valuations of things that are already built into our common language.[47] On the many occasions when we are pressed to join in denouncing or condemning this or that, we should, if possible, simply fail to respond.

That is about as far as I have yet been able to take my proposed reinvention of religious thought. It is an astonishingly slow, difficult and painful business. It has taken me many years, and that is all I have done. In the present essay I have been trying to understand a complication that has arisen: in recommending the direct and immediate solar commitment to life, I seem to be commending a strenuous ethic of living intensely and energetically. But how is this compatible with the fact that we moderns spend so much of our time dreaming about and lamenting lives that we missed living, kinsfolk who are lost to us in death, opportunities that we missed, unattainable ideals, and dead gods? We are much more aware than previous generations of all the roads that for one reason and another we did not take. Maybe I can learn to say "Amen" to the one contingent life that I have actually had; but I cannot help thinking that the one life I did live is surrounded by an indefinitely large number of other possible lives that might equally well have been mine if I had only happened to take different turns at various points along the road. And why do I cling to various religious and human loves that were never very practicable, and by now are permanently lost to me?

By way of an answer, let me point out what I think few have heretofore observed: namely, that the real world out there, a God-made, law-governed, finished work, was never just *given* to us. It was *an object of credal belief.* In the Creeds, it is "heaven and earth" or it is "all things visible and invisible." When dogmatic religion died and its God with it, the real world out there died too; it has been replaced by the humanly constructed world, a shifting, slightly fuzzy, consensus product.

In this process, our life changed radically. In the old God-made world your life was single. You had only one life-line, and it was created, predestined in the minutest detail, guarded, guided, and eventually ended by God. People knew nothing of the modern idea that one should try to take full control of, and responsibility for one's own life. God and God only controlled your life, and knew it all: when it began, how it was to be lived, when it would end. In a world ruled by the will of God, there was simply no reason to think about unfulfilled possibilities and missed life-chances. God's Will missed nothing. Your job was just to live out as your own the life that God had pre-programmed you to live.

Today, in our fuzzier man-made world, human life looks quite different. The one life I have actually lived is surrounded by an indefinitely large number of imaginary lives that I might well have lived, but happened not to. The gap between the contingently actual and the surrounding contingently non-actual is only very narrow. So I am driven to conclude that all our lost, missed, "impossible" loves are part of the truth about ourselves, and therefore it is not surprising that we should brood over them in our effort to make sense of our own lives.

A further and very tantalizing thought presents itself: I begin to suspect that in the new, emergent worldview the whole realm of "the Impossible" corresponds approximately to what the Supernatural realm was in the old worldview.[48] The actual life I, Don Cupitt, have lived is a single strand made up of a chain of contingencies, choices, misfortunes, and at least two outstanding bits of good fortune. It is surrounded by the whole realm of the Impossible, all the things that might once have been for me, but which now with the passage of time have become lost and impossible. Contemplating all these impossible loves, I feel the old pang, I smile wryly; but they do help me with the one vital task of learning how to end by being content with what I have been, what I have had, and what I have done, be it little or much.

APPENDIX

How long have we known?

My earlier suggestion (on p. 73, above) that all our lives we know about the basic facts of life—time, chance and death—raises the question of the precise age at which we first become aware of linear temporality and mortality. According to the Ernest Jones biography, Freud thought it was in early childhood, and such evidence as I can quickly consult supports that view. I was about five when I saw a dead dog by the side of the road, and knew instantly that this was the common fate of all living things—including me. In the same year I saw children collecting "pennies for the Guy," with a stuffed Guy Fawkes dummy sitting in an old bathchair. The dummy's head lolled, and I thought it was a dead man. And to cite another person's recollection, my wife was only three years old when one night her father went to bed as usual, but never got up again. A cerebral aneurysm burst in his head during the night, and next morning he was in a coma. He lingered only a very short while. The shocked child was for years afterwards afraid of the dark and afraid to fall asleep lest she too might never wake up.

Anecdotes such as these suggest that at least a general awareness of the limits of life lies in the background of our consciousness from a very early age. The popular view that it is not until the "mid-life crisis" of our forties or fifties that we seriously confront our own mortality seems to be mistaken, and fails to do justice to the seriousness of childhood thought.

First and Last Thoughts

The thoroughgoing reinvention of religion that I am proposing turns out to be, at its centre, very simple. (That is not surprising: I have been trying hard to make it as simple as I can.)

First we must make a single broad "cosmological" distinction, that between life in general and my life.

Second, we recognize that religion is a way of seeking to become reconciled to, and at ease with, life in general and one's own life in particular.

Third, we ask why there is need for reconciliation, and we reply that life is always subject to certain very general limits that can be summed up in the formula "Time, Chance, and Death." We fret against these limits and dream of being able to get around them, conquer them, or transcend them. But true religion finds salvation by choosing and affirming our life with all its limits as a package deal.

Fourth, we come to understand the good life as "solar" because (a) it is highly extravertive; (b) it achieves expressed selfhood only "retrospectively" and in passing; and (c) it seeks to add fresh value to the common world.

And finally, although the new religious life in our new world is a life of love, the self and its world are now so changeable and transient that all our loves have a poignant, "impossible" quality about them. Love always, irrationally, yearns for more than life can ever deliver to us. In this respect Love resembles both philosophical Reason and religious faith, both of which also yearn for a more complete, simultaneous, and secure fulfilment than they can ever in fact attain. Most of our religions, metaphysical systems, and love-poems dream of a culminating, absolute, intuitive, or visionary knowledge-through-love as the Supreme Goal of human life. But it is an impossible dream, as we should know by now. The highest wisdom, then, is to accept all this and to say, "I don't want to be an angel, and I don't ask for a world that is pure sweetness. I prefer to be a mortal, whose loves are bittersweet."

Two interesting questions remain to be answered. In sketching the intellectual and religious core of a new Second-Axial-Age vision of the human world, one around which a new culture may one day be built, am I going back to foundationalism and perhaps even back to metaphysics? Am I perhaps still irretrievably caught up in the old ways of thinking from which we are all nowadays trying to break free?

In reply, I think I just have to accept what Nietzsche, Wittgenstein, and Derrida all acknowledged: that a complete break with the past and an absolutely fresh start are not really possible. I have tried to write in a way that foresees and disarms this obvious challenge, but I know that like everyone else I cannot help but bring some baggage with me into the new age.

The second question is much more difficult. I have gone a very long way back in my attempt to find a platform, a stable religious centre or core of acceptance and reconciliation around which the culture of the future may be built. I have gone back to a point before the cultural distinctions between reason and nonreason, and between sanity and madness; before truth, before objectivity, before reality. But when I try to go back as far as that, what sort of rightness or appropriateness or "weak truth" can I claim for the ideas I am putting forward? Remember that in the broadly postmodern worldview that I describe everything is permanently in flux, and there is no "ground" of any sort: no firm ground, no common ground, no ground on which to get a footing. Everything is floating. So how can I pretend to have "got it right" in any sense? Dare I claim that the religious way I have described is, in some minimal sense, *rational*?

I answer that I see the job of religion as being simply and minimally to enable us to bear life: it helps us feel that we can go on, that the human enterprise is worth continuing with, that we have just about enough calm and enough space to build a culture.

Look again at my minimal cosmology of "life" and "my life." This is pretty unmetaphysical. I am not committed to belief in either the world or the self, but only life and my life. And the distinction is made only in order to reunite the terms—as the old maxim has it, *distinguer pour unir*. My very simple pre-reason and pre-sanity is a basic feeling of coherence, fit, and harmony between the process of my own life and the larger stream of life of which I am part. And when I say that religion is about reconciling us to ourselves and to life in general, I am again thinking of religion as something that calms us down and opens a comfortably large and peaceful space in which something good can be built.

I am not, of course, claiming anything like the Cartesian *cogito ergo sum*. I am looking only for some new *first thoughts* that I hope may satisfy doubters and persuade people that a future reconstruction of the human world will be possible. Maybe. One day.

Notes

Chapter One: So Far

1. See *The New Religion of Life in Everyday Speech*, *The Meaning of It All in Everyday Speech*, and *Kingdom Come in Everyday Speech*. The discussion was taken a stage further by a second little trilogy, *Life, Life*, *The Way to Happiness*, and *The Great Questions of Life*. See also *The Old Creed and the New*.

2. *Solar Ethics.*

3. Gellner, *Legitimation of Belief*, 28f.

4. Heelas and Woodhead, *The Spiritual Revolution: Why religion is giving way to spirituality.*

5. Notice that in his ode "On Time" John Milton apostrophizes Time, Chance, and Death as our great enemies, which we hope in the end to see conquered. I hold that there is no sense in the suggestion that we could see them "conquered" while yet being and remaining ourselves. We have to learn to live with them. At this point my religion differs sharply from Milton's, and from all traditional faith.

6. "Green and dying" is a phrase from Dylan Thomas's "Fern Hill"; "The more I give, the more I have" is from *Romeo and Juliet*.

7. I now think Tolstoy anticipated my view. See how Ivan Illych in the great *novella* is able to die happy when he can carry his affirmation of life right into the moment of his own death.

8. See *The Way to Happiness.*

Chapter Two: Love for the Dead

9. Rundle, *Why there is Something rather than Nothing.*

10. Kierkegaard, *Works of Love*, Part 2, chap. 9.

Chapter Three: Great Love and Eternal Separation

11. Here I presume that *Wuthering Heights* is so familiar that no detailed references are needed.

12. For Strelley, see Pevsner, *The Buildings of England: Nottinghamshire*, 338ff. and Plate 43.

13. For Lowick and the Greenes, see Pevsner, *The Buildings of England: Northamptonshire*, 297f. and Plate 51. In his poem "An Arundel Tomb" Philip

Larkin finds and describes a third example, but I have not yet identified and examined the monument he has in mind.

Chapter Four: Love for a Dead God

14. Gill, ed., *William Wordsworth: The Major Works*, 334 and 720n.

15. Williams, ed., *Thomas Hardy*, 95f.

16. This brief discussion of Derrida is much indebted to Rayment-Pickard, *Impossible God: Derrida's Theology*.

17. Derrida, *Of Grammatology*, 14.

18. I Cor 13:12.

19. The phrase "conspicuous by one's absence" was, I am informed, introduced into modern English by the politician Lord John Russell in 1859. He seems to have taken it from Tacitus, *Annals*, iii.76.

Chapter Five: Loves Lost or Out of the Question

20. Two well-known novels that have dealt with this topic are Luke Rheinhart's *The Dice Man* and Iris Murdoch's *An Accidental Man* (both 1971).

21. The Book of Common Prayer's Collect for the Fourth Sunday after the Epiphany.

22. The classical source of speculations of this kind is the philosophy of Leibniz, who pictured God as reviewing all possible worlds before deciding to actualize the one that is all in all best.

23. Universalism, the strongest form of the doctrine of apocatastasis, taught universal salvation and was eventually condemned as heretical. But the orthodox doctrine of God's infinite power and goodness seems to require at the very least a moderate form of apocatastasis to obtain at the "end of the world."

24. A phrase from *Twelfth Night*.

Chapter Six: The Impossible Ideal

25. In the age of structuralism, these ideas were classically explained by the anthropologist Mary Douglas, esp. in her well-known book *Purity and Danger*. See also her *Natural Symbols*.

Chapter Seven: Life as a Chapter of Accidents

26. Ghiselin, *The Triumph of the Darwinian Method* is memorable for its exposition of how thoroughly Darwin considered and demolished the then current ideas of "intelligent design" in Nature.

27. Lawson, *Closure: A Story of Everything*, discusses these themes in a manner I find very congenial.

Chapter Eight: The Impossible and the Supernatural

28. In *Spectres of Marx* and other later works Derrida uses terms such as "hauntology" and "spectrality" in this connexion. Usually I like neologisms, but I think I will refrain from adopting these two.

29. The point that a prohibition cannot help but remind us vividly of what has been prohibited is well illustrated by the case of Erostratos, who burnt the

Temple of Diana at Ephesus in order to ensure that his own name would live. Incensed, the city authorities tried to defeat Erostratos' ambition by forbidding mention of his name—and the prohibition naturally helped to keep Erostratos' name alive.

30. Several of our contemporaries in Britain, such as Philip Pullman and Richard Dawkins, are good examples of God-haunted atheism. The close analogy between God and a dead human person (both live in the spiritual world "up there" and in our heads; both are benign and unchanging, and "look down" upon us; both are talked to but don't talk back, etc.) was pointed out quite independently twenty years ago in Williams, *Ethics and the Limits of Philosophy*, 33.

31. Quotations are from the RSV.

32. The finite anthropomorphic sky-God is still the God Milton must work with in *Paradise Lost*, the God painted by Michaelangelo, and the God of much popular belief to this day.

Chapter Nine: Aimless Love

33. In the age of belief in God and of metaphysics generally, the child-to-parent relation also had great cosmological significance; but that has recently been lost.

34. My account of aimless love is intended to replace the Christian notion of agapeistic love, which I now think is untruthful and of little use to us.

Some readers may comment that aimless love has always been a recognized possibility in our culture, and that the special mutual feeling of twins has long been the standard symbol of it. Hence "twin souls"; and note that the twins of classical mythology, Castor and Pollux, were demigods, the "Dioscuri" (children of Zeus), who divided their time between heaven and Hades. Around the world it has been very widely felt that there is something magical or supernatural about twins—so much so that many children have invented an invisible twin companion for themselves. And such an invisible playmate must be an aimless love.

Well, maybe: but I'd like to try to get aimless love out of that context and see it become "normal" and socially accepted. Two possible forerunners of it were considered perfectly acceptable in their own day, namely the brother-sister relationship in the Romantic period, and exceptionally strong friendship between men in High Victorian times.

Chapter Ten: That's the Story of My Life

35. This rather good image was used by A. O. Lovejoy in his classic study of the history of ideas, *The Great Chain of Being* (1936). Kierkegaard's use of the pseudonym "Climacus" shows that he was aware that he was himself translating the traditional Ladder of Divine Ascent into a succession of stages in the life of a modern person.

36. For the rise of the modern self, see Taylor, *Sources of the Self: The Making of the Modern Identity*.

37. A very good exponent of these themes was the English painter Patrick Heron, a Matisse admirer who opposed "conceptual art" and remained loyal to what he called "sensationalism" on the grounds that painting is and should

remain about color and visual pleasure. Amen to that. See Gooding, *Patrick Heron*.

38. As Rachel Muers pointed out while the book was still being written: see *Solar Ethics*, 17.

39. In my Sea of Faith (UK) Conference Lecture for 2004, unpublished but currently accessible via the Sea of Faith (UK) website at www.sofn.org.uk, and see p. 62, above.

40. Derrida, *Apprendre à Vivre Enfin: Entretien avec Jean Birnbaum*. The interview took place just two months before Derrida's death.

41. See my *The Way to Happiness*.

Chapter Eleven: Sweet Sorrow

42. E.g., Hos 11:1–9.

Chapter Twelve: Religion after the West

43. Spengler, *The Decline of the West*, 1918–22.

44. The term "mediascape" is Jean Baudrillard's. For a good short discussion of his view of the mass media see Kellner, *Jean Baudrillard: From Marxism to Postmodernism and Beyond*, chap. 3.

45. A people's material culture is the whole array of material goods they produce, including housing, clothing, pottery, weapons etc. Their ideal culture is in a broad sense symbolic, and includes their language and their social institutions, such as religion, law, worldview, and art.

46. The ideas summarized in the following paragraphs were first introduced in various of my recent books, including *Life, Life*, *The Way to Happiness*, and *The Great Questions of Life*, as well as *The Old Creed and the New*.

A further comment is needed on why I have chosen to make my new beginning with the distinction between *life* and *my life*. The first need of the pre-socratic philosophers was to establish a secular, non-mythological conception of the world, so that is what most of them started by doing. We today find ourselves in a very different position, for we already have very grand and highly developed systems of scientific knowledge. Science is by far our greatest achievement, and I don't propose to tamper with it. Our problem is to understand and to "place" in the world all the things that science presupposes and leaves unthought; that is, we need basic, simple conceptions of the first-person subject "myself," and how it fits into and plays its part in the living world of human language and communication within which in turn scientific knowledge is constructed.

The life/my life distinction was first suggested to me by my study of the word "life" in the years 1998–2003. Gradually, I came to see how powerful and interesting it is as a "first thought," and hence the part it plays in the present essay.

47. These ideas go all the way back to 1988 and my book *The New Christian Ethics*.

48. Here is a puzzle: Kierkegaard takes up a saying that occurs several times in the Gospels of Matthew and Mark to the effect that for the believer all things

are possible with God, and seems to equate God with the whole sphere of "the possible." Derrida, by contrast, has a theology of God's *im*possibility. What's going on here?

Kierkegaard, I think, is contrasting the knowable, fixed past with the future—which is open and unknowable, and into which we must walk by faith. Derrida is making a different point altogether: he is saying that even the most militant atheism can never finally rid itself of God, not even when it shows that God is impossible; for God still returns as a kind of haunting absence. Even when dead, God won't lie down.

In the well-known essay "Circumfession" (see Bennington, *Jacques Derrida*, 3) Derrida says that he has "never loved anything but the impossible." This means that it is the very nature of love always to demand more than reality (such as it is) can ever deliver. In that sense all loves are "impossible," and the love of God is the supreme example and symbol of love's divine absurdity and impossibility. On which note I can close this book, reassured that by reading this footnote you have demonstrated that you have stayed with me.

Bibliography

Bennington, Geoffrey. *Jacques Derrida*. Chicago: University of Chicago Press, 1993.

Cupitt, Don. *The Great Questions of Life*. Santa Rosa, CA: Polebridge Press, 2006.

————. *Kingdom Come in Everyday Speech*. London: SCM Press, 2000.

————. *Life Lines*. London: SCM Press, 1986.

————. *Life, Life*. Santa Rosa, CA: Polebridge Press, 2003

————. *The Meaning of It All in Everyday Speech*. London: SCM Press, 1999.

————. *The New Christian Ethics*. London: SCM Press, 1988.

————. *The New Religion of Life in Everyday Speech*. London: SCM Press, 1999.

————. *The Old Creed and the New*. London: SCM Press, 2006.

————. *Solar Ethics*. London: SCM Press, 1995.

————. *The Way to Happiness*. Santa Rosa, CA: Polebridge Press, 2005.

Derrida, Jacques. *Apprendre à Vivre Enfin: Entretien avec Jean Birnbaum*. Paris: Galilee/Le Monde, 2005.

————. *Of Grammatology*. Translated by Gayatri Spivak. Baltimore, MD: Johns Hopkins University Press, 1976.

————. *Spectres of Marx*. New York: Routledge, 1994.

Douglas, Mary. *Natural Symbols*. Harmondsworth: Pelican Books, 1973.

————. *Purity and Danger*. London: Routledge, 1966.

Gellner, Ernest. *Legitimation of Belief*. Cambridge: The Cambridge University Press 1974.pp.28f.

Ghiselin, M. T. *The Triumph of the Darwinian Method*. Berkeley: University of California Press, 1969.

Gill, Stephen, editor. *William Wordsworth: The Major Works*. Oxford World's Classics, 2000.

Gooding, Mel. *Patrick Heron*. London: Phaidon Press, 1994.

Heelas, Paul, and Linda Woodhead, *The Spiritual Revolution: Why religion is giving way to spirituality*. Oxford and Malden, MA: Blackwell, 2005.

Kellner, Douglas. *Jean Baudrillard: From Marxism to Postmodernism and Beyond*. Cambridge: Polity Press, 1989.

Lawson, Hilary. *Closure: A Story of Everything.* London and New York:
    Routledge, 2001.
Lovejoy. A. O. *The Great Chain of Being: A Study of the History of an Idea.*
    Cambridge, MA, Harvard University Press, 1936.
Pevsner, Nikolaus. *The Buildings of England: Northamptonshire.* Second
    edition. Revised by Bridget Cherry. Harmondsworth: Penguin Books
    1973.
_____. *The Buildings of England: Nottinghamshire.* Second edition. Re-
    vised by Elizabeth Williamson. Harmondsworth: Penguin Books 1979.
Rayment-Pickard, Hugh. *Impossible God: Derrida's Theology.* Aldershot
    and Burlington, VT: Ashgate, 2003.
Rundle, Bede. *Why there is Something rather than Nothing.* Oxford: the
    Clarendon Press, 2004.
Spengler, Oswald. *The Decline of the West.* Authorized translation with
    notes by Charles Francis Atkinson. New York: A. A. Knopf, 1926–28.
Taylor, Charles. *Sources of the Self: The Making of the Modern Identity.*
    Cambridge: The Cambridge University Press, 1989.
Williams, Bernard. *Ethics and the Limits of Philosophy.* London: Fontana,
    1985.
Williams, W. E., editor. *Thomas Hardy: A selection of poems chosen and
    edited by W. E. Williams.* Harmondsworth: Penguin Books, 1960.

Index

Don Cupitt is a Life Fellow and former Dean of Emmanuel College, Cambridge, England, and the author of more than thirty books including, *Life, Life* (2003), *The Way to Happiness* (2005), and *The Great Questions of Life* (2006). A frequent broadcaster, mainly for the BBC, he has made three TV Series, one of which, "The Sea of Faith," (1984), gave rise to a book and to an international network of radical Christians which is still growing.